Faith Through The Darkness
Based on a true story

By: Ryan Curtis

Dedicated to the Author of Faith
and Worker of Miracles.

RYAN CURTIS BOOKS

BOOKS THAT ENTERTAIN AND INSPIRE

© 2017 Ryan Curtis Books

Ryan Curtis Books,
ryan(at)ryancurtisbooks.com

Printed by CreateSpace

ISBN - 978-1546905462

Cover art by Andrew Brown

Notice: This book is based on a true story, though some facts and details have been changed, omitted and otherwise manipulated to protect identities and avoid conflict. This is a novel and should be treated as such, though I have tried to convey the truth as I learned it.

Contents

For more inspiring stories and books from Ryan Curtis, please follow his blog at

www.ryancurtisbooks.com.

Ryan has also written, *Love Like Alzheimer's* - a novel about how a young couple faces the challenge of taking advantage of the time they have with their grandma who has Alzheimer's disease. You will learn about the disease and how caregivers can cope.

Don't forget to leave a review of *Faith Through The Darkness* on Goodreads, Amazon and your favorite eBook stores.

Introduction
Dream-Vision

July 2009, 3:00 a.m.

Amanda woke from her sleep, her pulse beating rapidly. Not knowing what caused her to wake up, she sat up in her bed.

Though the room was dark, Amanda saw a vivid scene play out in her mind.

She was sitting on the passenger side of a vehicle driven by her friend. They were talking and heading down a major highway that was on high ground. Off to the right, Amanda could see a city. She could see that a storm was forming in the distance behind the city. As she looked at the buildings, she saw her three children - Jacob, Jackson, and Ally - standing on a street corner. They were alone.

Amanda's mind raced to make sense of the situation. What are they doing down there? What's going on?

As she looked beyond where her kids were standing, she noticed that there was a giant tornado ripping through the city. It was coming straight for her kids.

In a panic, Amanda told her friend to stop the car, so she could get to her children. As she tried to frantically unbuckle her seat belt and unlock the door, her friend said, "You'll never make it in time."

"Pull over anyway," Amanda pleaded, wishing and hoping a solution would present itself. She jumped out of the car and looked at her kids. The storm was perilously close, and she was too far away from them.

Her heart nearly stopped beating for the hurt she felt. She

could see the utter destruction that lay beyond the tornado. In fact, there was nothing but blackness in the wake of that awful cyclone. Her kids were right in its path with no one to help them. She saw that this was inevitably the end of their short lives.

Still not wanting to give up, but seeing that she could do nothing to stop the inevitable, she did the only thing she could think of ... pray.

She looked to heaven, and cried out, "God, please help my kids!"

Almost immediately, she saw a pillar of light pierce the clouds, and Jesus descended on the city. He came down between Amanda's kids and the destructive tornado. Facing the storm, He opened His arms, and the storm began to shrink. He was absorbing the cyclone's energy. The next thing she knew, the tempest was gone. The sky began to grow brighter and she knew her kids were safe.

Christ turned to Amanda and her three kids and said, "Don't be afraid. I am watching over you and will save you."

Just as suddenly as it started, it stopped.

Amanda was once again sitting in her room at 3:00 am.

She hadn't been dreaming because she remembered waking up, but it also wasn't a figment of her imagination. What was it? She wondered if it was about the divorce and the turmoil it had caused for her family. The divorce had happened two years earlier. The kids seemed to be adjusting as well as could be hoped for in that situation so it probably wasn't that. She laid there for at least an hour, but sleep eluded her as she thought about the strange vision she had seen. *What could it mean?* she asked herself.

In the morning, she woke from a fitful sleep. She quickly put on her robe and went to her kids. Jacob and Jackson were already up and were playing together with their toy tractors on the floor. Ally wasn't up yet. Amanda grabbed her 9-year-old and 7-year-old and hugged them in silence for at least a full minute.

"What's wrong, Momma?" Jacob asked as he searched her face. Jackson looked at her for a moment and then went back to his tractor.

Amanda told her boys about the vision. They were as puzzled as she was.

"I don't know what it means, but promise me that you two will be extra careful," Amanda said, taking her boys in her arms again. The she continued. "Look both ways before crossing the street, and don't talk to strangers. We have to make sure we watch out for Ally too."

Amanda ran to her daughter's room. Her precious daughter was starting to stir when Amanda came to the room. Ally was nearly 3-years-old. She gave her mother a brief smile as she started to sit up. Amanda wrapped her daughter in her arms, and they hugged in silence until Ally asked for breakfast.

After she had got her kids something to eat, Amanda took her phone and went into her bedroom. She called her pastor, Brother Ratley, and told him and his wife about what she had experienced.

"Something is going to happen," Amanda said, her emotions evident in her voice. "It's going to be OK, but I feel like it's not OK. It's like God is warning me, and something is going to happen to my family. I'm scared."

"But it had a good ending, right?" came the motherly response from Sister Ratley.

Try as she might, Amanda couldn't quiet her fears. For days she continued to ponder what it could mean. Was something going to happen to all three kids? Was it just going to happen to one child? Each moment of pondering quickly brought the graphic images back to her mind. Each time she would pray, "God, please don't let anything happen to my kids. Don't let it be something we can't deal with or handle together as a family."

Her paranoia ran high for a week, then a little less for two weeks. She began to relax a little after four weeks. Her anxiety slowly diminished over time, but she spent every reasonable opportunity, and a few unreasonable opportunities, cautioning her children to be careful and safe. Life eventually took over, and Amanda rarely thought about the vision after six months had passed.

Chapter 1

Sunday Dinner

June 6, 2010

Amanda was cooking Sunday dinner for her three children in their red-brick rental house. This meal was a special time for Amanda. She was a good cook and Sundays were an important day for her, but she loved it because she could focus on spending time with her kids.

Most weeks they would go to church and spend time together during the day. Amanda would cook a nice meal, and they would sit and talk. Some weeks they would go to a family member's house for dinner. No matter where she was, she just wanted to be present with her kids and not worry about anything else. Maybe that's why she looked forward to Sunday dinner.

As a single mother of three, she had to take her boys to school, and take her daughter to daycare. She worked a full-time job, and at one point it was an hour commute. She had to keep up with the chores around the rental house and study so she could finish an associate's degree. She had managed the paperwork and accounting for her ex-husband's farm before the divorce. After they seperated but before she finished her college degree, she couldn't find any decent jobs in her small town. Once she completed her associate's degree in business administration in 2008, she was able to find a job working for an insurance agency. She sold insurance under the owner but was studying to become a licensed insurance agent. This was one of the better jobs she could get in the small community of

Forest, Louisiana, a small town roughly 10 miles from the Mississippi River in the northeastern portion of the state.

Amanda's previous marriage provided material comfort but often left her feeling empty and scared. Her main goal now was to create a safe home for herself and the kids. Her ex-husband was a farmer who worked several thousand acres in the surrounding area. He had done well for himself because he worked a lot. He wasn't home much, but when he was his anger flared at the drop of a hat. She had wanted to avoid a long drawn out court battle, so she settled out of court. She didn't require alimony, just child support. She maintained custody of the children, but they agreed the kids would visit their father every other weekend. Despite trying to keep it civil, the divorce was still ugly and painful with a lot of emotional scars.

Amanda had finished cooking dinner and asked Jacob to help set the table. Jacob was 10 years old and had a loving heart. He was going to be tall like his father. Amanda was only five feet four inches tall. Jacob was four feet seven inches tall and about the same weight as his mother. Right now the boys were playing on the floor with their tractors and cars. He answered Amanda's request with a polite, "Yes, Ma'am." He was easy going and unrushed as usual. He came to the kitchen and grabbed the plates and cups and put them on the table.

Jacob was growing up so quickly. As the oldest, Jacob understood the most about the divorce that separated his parents, though he was only seven at the time. Amanda hadn't seen him cry much about it, but he clung to her more than he had before. Life had made him mature quickly, but Amanda was proud of the little man he was becoming.

As she watched them play, she reflected on the simplicity of the moment. They didn't have a care in the world. They were in their own special place of trucks and tractors. Amanda had driven tractors while she was pregnant with Jacob. Jacob's first word was "tractor." He loved tractors and farming.

Amanda asked Jackson to take the silverware to the table. He was already up before she had asked. When he heard her ask Jacob to help, he was anxious to come and help too. So when Amanda asked Jackson to get the silverware, he was nearly in the kitchen already and said, "Yes, Ma'am." He grabbed the silverware out of the drawer and put it on the table, distributing them at the various place settings.

Jackson was anxious to keep up with his brother or pass him if he could. Though he was two years younger, he wanted to do everything with his brother, and they were rarely apart. Jackson was coming into his own personality, and Amanda knew she needed to give him individual attention. She laughed to herself when she watched Jackson sometimes. He was spontaneous, had a good mind, but he was fearless.

Jacob and Jackson didn't call each other by their first names, they would simply call each other, "brother." It meant a lot to them to have each other, so the relationship and bond were stronger than names. Brother watched out for brother, and that was that. They fought like cats and dogs sometimes, but they loved each other all the time.

Amanda brought over the chicken, rolls and collard greens and set them on the table. Ally was nearly four years old. She had busied herself that Sunday afternoon with a doll she dressed up. She would frequently stop to check on Amanda's progress with dinner and join her brothers in their play for a time. Now she climbed up into her chair to inspect the meal with pleasure.

With the table set, everyone took their usual places: Amanda on one end, Jacob on the other, with Jackson and Ally sitting on the side. The kitchen/dining room was too small to allow them to use all four sides of the table, so they put it against the wall and made do with three.

As Amanda sat at the table eating, she thought to herself, *soon things will slow down a little, and I can enjoy my family a little more.*

As she thought this, Jacob started talking about their

float trip they took a few years earlier. It had been a warm summer day before the divorce. Amanda wanted to take her boys outdoors, and their father was too busy to go with them. Amanda had packed lunches and drinks in a cooler. They went to the river and put the cooler on a tube. Then Amanda, Jacob, and Jackson got in tubes and floated on the water all afternoon.

The boys laughed about how they splashed each other in the water, and how they almost lost the cooler. When Jacob teased Jackson about how he reacted when he thought a fish had touched him, Ally laughed too, though she had not been there. Amanda joined in with her own memories of that float trip. Everyone was happy.

Soon, Amanda thought, *we will be able to take some time to go camping or something.*

They loved to be outdoors, and Amanda enjoyed the clarity she felt when she was there. Long before the divorce, she put a premium on making memories with her kids. She knew she needed to make time for them to do things together. She needed to build a strong relationship with her kids. Especially when her relationship with their father had been falling apart, she wanted her children to know they were loved. Even now, with all the chaos in their lives and little resources, a little camping trip together was time well spent. It was almost like God was telling her, "This is what I want you to focus on. These kids are what's important, not possessions or money."

Amanda had always put her kids above money or stuff, but since the divorce, time seemed as scarce as money. She had to really try and make time for the kids. She had to support them financially, but it was a means, not the end. That's why Sunday dinner was so important. It helped her take a break from the week, and give her kids attention without any interruptions.

Chapter 2

House Hunting

When Amanda set her heart on buying a house, she knew a few things. It would have to accommodate at least three kids and herself. She didn't care if it was new or fancy, but it needed to be affordable. That last hurdle was proving to be the more difficult requirement.

It had taken her three years of living in a cramped rental for Amanda to save up enough money on a down payment for a small house - a place she could call her own. She had decided that if she could save up $10,000, she could look for a house. Last November that goal was accomplished, and Amanda talked to the bank. She wanted to make sure her loan amount was low enough that she could make the payments comfortably with her current job. If she lost her job or needed to change jobs, she would still be able to make the payments with most jobs that were available in the area.

Once she was pre-approved for a home loan, Amanda started looking for a house. She had looked in communities that were farther away, but for one reason or another - family or finances - she couldn't make it work. In order to save money, Amanda didn't hire a real estate agent. She had to watch the newspapers and community websites for house listings. Life didn't slow down just because she wanted to find a home. After months of not finding much within her price range, she saw a house for sale by owner that was just across the street from the school where her kids were enrolled. She went over and talked to the owners about the house. It was a three bedroom, tan brick house with four white columns in front. They wanted just less than she was pre-approved for. She thought it would work out nicely for her family, especially since it was close to school and her work. It wasn't a dump, and it wasn't a fancy, high-priced home. It was going to fit their family for a while, and she could afford it.

Amanda ordered inspections, negotiated the price, and worked with her bank on the loan. She scheduled the closing with the title company and handled all the duties a real estate agent normally would do. It was a lot of work and some days it wore her out, but it was a worthwhile sacrifice. The family that sold the house was still living in it so Amanda's family couldn't move in until the first of July.

It was now the second Thursday in June. She was with seven of her closest friends. Usually, they had twelve women that would try to make these game nights. These women were nearly sisters. They stuck together through everything. Amanda had been able to lean on some of them frequently during her divorce. She had been there for one of the other women when she lost her mother to breast cancer. Any time one of the group had a problem or just needed a shoulder to cry on, they were there.

One evening each month they would get together to play Pokeno, eat dinner and chat. Pokeno is like bingo but played with face cards. It was a simple diversion, but one all of them needed from time to time. They would rotate around to different houses so they all would get to host the two-hour get-together. The host would cook dinner, and sometimes that meant elaborate preparations, but that wasn't a requirement on the host.

"How is the house closing coming, Amanda?" Rebecca asked as Whitney shuffled the cards to start a new game.

"It's been crazy, but we close on the house next week - on Monday," Amanda said while switching out her Pokeno card. "It will be nice to have it over with. I'm excited to have a place of my own."

"That's wonderful," Rebecca said first, then the others echoed the sentiment.

"I don't know how you do it, Amanda," said Amber. "I thought buying our house with a realtor was a lot of work."

"You've handled all the inspections and everything yourself?" asked Whitney. "When we bought a house, it seemed like one thing after another had to be done before we could sign our lives away at closing. I didn't want to know all the details, but Mike just insisted that he tell me everything."

"Oh, it was a lot of work, but it's done now," Amanda said. "I don't want to do it again for a long time, but it will be nice to have a place of my own."

"When are you moving?" Rebecca asked. "Do you need help?"

"I think we will be able to manage," Amanda said with a dismissive wave of her hand. "We don't have that much stuff. We were planning to move in on the second or third of July. The kids can help me move some things, and then they will be at their dad's for two weeks. I will have a little time with just Ally when I can get things situated."

"Is everyone ready for another round?" Whitney asked.

They started the game and kept discussing things that were going on in their lives. Each finding support from others. Amanda always felt strengthened when she left those game nights. Not because of what was said, but because she knew they would be there for her. She also heard what everyone else was struggling through and it helped her realize that she could make it through her own problems.

Chapter 3
Moving In

On July 3, Amanda and her kids packed their belongings to move into their new home. The excitement and stress were almost more than Amanda could bear. She would finally have a place of her own. She was also glad the process was nearly complete.

She had ordered inspections and followed up with repairs. She signed her name to a ream of paper, it seemed and then had to pack up her rental house. If that were all she had to do it wouldn't be so bad, but she was still working 40 hours a week, studying for her insurance license and coordinating child care.

Her life had also developed a new wrinkle. In the middle of June, the kids started a summer schedule. They would spend two weeks with their father and then come home for a week. Their father thought this would help balance out the time he missed during the school year when he only got to see his kids every other weekend. It was actually just the boys that were going with their father during the week because Ally was too young to be out on the farm all day.

Amanda missed the boys terribly the first time they went to be with their father for 14 days. Amanda had been able to spend a little more time with Ally, but it was hard to not have the family together. The rest of the summer would be even more difficult for her because she would be done with her test, and she hoped life would slow down a little. She would have more time to miss her boys.

Amanda handed both Jacob and Jackson a box. Then she

grabbed a box herself and went out to her Expedition. She hadn't needed a moving truck since they didn't have a lot of large items or a ton of personal belongings. Rebecca had shown up even though Amanda hadn't asked her to come. Two cousins and her father had shown up with pickup trucks and helped her move beds and other furniture to her new house. They were able to make it in one load.

As they drove to the house, Jacob asked, "Are we going to do any fireworks for the Fourth of July this year?"

"We're going to do fireworks with your cousins," Amanda replied.

She was relieved that she didn't have to worry about doing fireworks on her own. As it was, she had almost forgotten about Independence Day. She had just spent a week with all her kids together again, and it had flown by. Amanda had been burning the candle at both ends all week. They would have to spend the rest of Saturday and Sunday unpacking boxes, but they would make time for fun. She would take the two weeks they were with their dad to get the house situated. It would also give her something to do to help pass the time.

Amanda looked in the rear view mirror at Jackson. He was looking out the window with a slight smile on his face. The boys were excited about mom's new house. They were fine with still sharing a room. Ally didn't really understand, but she was excited because her mom and brothers were excited.

Once at the house, Amanda, her kids and their family and friends, unpacked the boxes and furniture. Dressers and beds were put in temporary spots, as Amanda wanted to paint rooms before everything was put away. The previous owner had painted over some paneling on the walls. Amanda thought the paneling looked tacky, but she wasn't interested in removing the surface to get down to the drywall. Instead, Amanda decided to texture the walls to hide the paneling. Then she was going to paint the walls blue for the boys. It would be a project she just had to take a day at a time, though. For now, Amanda had to focus on unpacking the kitchen boxes so they would be able to eat lunch.

"You're still coming over for dinner tonight, right?" Rebecca said, as Amanda pulled out boxes of food and put them in the pantry.

"Thank you, but you don't have to do that," Amanda said, worried it would mess up Rebecca's plans to feed her family too. "I'm sure I will find a skillet around here soon, and then I can make dinner."

"And break my kids' hearts?" Rebecca argued. "You better not. Our kids can play together, and you need a break. I know you won't stop working if you don't leave for a little bit. So come over and eat and then you can come back and continue unpacking."

The weekend passed just as quickly as the week before it. They only got the essentials unpacked before heading over to Rebecca's. The next day, Amanda and her kids went to church and celebrated the Fourth of July with food, family, friends and fireworks. Jacob loved the barbecue and corn. Jackson had a second helping of potato salad, and Ally got watermelon juice all over her shirt. They had a good time.

Unfortunately for Amanda, they had to meet up with the kids' father right after the fireworks. He and the boys had to be up early to work on the farm. Amanda hugged Ally as the boys left. She felt some frustration that her kids had to be gone for two weeks, but she didn't want to linger on those thoughts. She smiled at Ally and took her home to their new house.

On Monday, Jacob sent a silly picture and a text saying, "I love you!" Then Tuesday he sent a couple more texts. Wednesday evening he sent another silly picture and a funny explanation. In a week, Jacob had sent more tender texts and fun pictures than he had ever done before while on a visit with his dad.

"He must be feeling homesick, or something," Amanda said to herself. "He's so sweet."

Chapter 4
Casual Friday

"Mom, I miss you. I'm ready to come home," read the text Amanda got at 6:00 am. It was Jacob.

Amanda looked at the text. It had been nearly two weeks since her boys went to stay with their dad. Their day started early, usually around 5:00 am, and went until about 11:00 pm. She wasn't surprised that Jacob was texting her at this time in the morning. She had given the boys a cell phone to share when they went to stay with their dad. Amanda didn't want to talk to her ex-husband any more than necessary, so she made sure she had a direct line to the boys.

"I miss you too," Amanda texted back. "You will be home soon."

Amanda wanted to bring Jacob and Jackson home a long time ago. This new schedule was hard on everyone, especially towards the end of the two weeks. Amanda was torn. She wanted to be fair to the kids and to their father, but she also wanted to have her kids home with her. It wouldn't help to say that to Jacob though.

Then in an attempt to change the subject, she texted, "Your room is painted."

Amanda had been able to paint the kids' rooms and set up the kitchen, but she hadn't been able to set up bunk beds or arrange dressers yet.

"Cool. Can I come home and help?" was Jacob's immediate response. He was looking for a reason to come home. He might be just excited about setting up his new room, or maybe it was the intense, constant heat he had been in for 11 days now.

No matter how badly she wanted her boys home, she didn't want to make them more miserable, so she texted, "I love You!" and put down her phone. She had to focus on getting ready for work and getting Ally to daycare.

Casual Friday would be in effect today, so Amanda looked for something fun to wear. She chose a denim, knee-length skirt with a red and white striped top. *I look a little patriotic today,* she mused to herself as she looked in the mirror. For shoes, she went with leather flip-flops.

Amanda worked for a local insurance company. She had been there for a year now and had just finished the property and casualty insurance course so she could schedule her insurance agent test. As an agent, she would have more responsibility and better pay. She had to drive to Shreveport to take the test, and that meant a two and a half hour drive.

"Next Wednesday is the big day," Amanda said to herself. Then thinking about the day of travel and taking the test, she realized she wouldn't see any of her kids much that day. "Maybe I can get their dad to let me have the children a day early now if he can get them again on Wednesday while I drive to Shreveport to take the test?"

She could easily have her grandma watch them or even a friend. It might be easier to just use a friend rather than get into trading days and negotiating time. She would probably only be gone 8 hours or so. *I'll decide later,* she mused to herself.

After she was ready, she got Ally dressed. Ally wanted a skirt, just like mommy. Amanda was glad she had Ally with her all the time. These two-week increments when the boys were gone gave Amanda a lot more one-on-one time with her daughter. When Ally was dressed, Amanda took her to daycare in her white Expedition.

Before heading into the office, Amanda went home to take care of a few things. As she got ready to walk back out the door to go to work, something didn't feel right. It was as if something were missing. She reached up to her neck and realized she didn't have on any jewelry. She liked jewelry but didn't always wear a necklace. Today was different. It almost seemed necessary. She went back in the house and looked through her jewelry box.

Amanda picked up a couple necklaces that she wore a lot and considered them. She needed to hurry, but she wasn't in the mood for wearing those. Then she saw towards the bottom a chain she hadn't worn in at least two years. It was a gift, but she couldn't remember who gave it to her.

The necklace was a simple gold chain with a small cross. On the cross were a few small diamonds down the middle and across the upper beam. As she looked at it now, this piece of jewelry just seemed perfect. She grabbed it and left for work. The necklace was so knotted, it took her five minutes to untangle it.

Jacob and Jackson were with their father on some rural land just north of the Arkansas-Louisiana border where their father farmed rented land. Today, their dad and workers would be leveling the fields in preparation for planting. The sun beat down on them. Summer in that humid, southern part of the country was unforgiving. The heat was more than 110 degrees outside, without the heat index. Farmers work hard from sunup to sundown, and sometimes later. Jacob and Jackson rode along but didn't do the work yet. They sat on tractors or in fields for nearly 16 hours a day. The tractors were newer and had air conditioning, a saving grace for the two boys most days.

With little to do with the farming at 10 years of age, Jacob was texting Amanda frequently throughout this Friday morning.

"Please call dad and ask him if we can go home," he begged.

"Just tell him you need my help," he messaged 10 minutes later. "I'll mow the yard ... fold laundry ... whatever."

"We'll see," was all Amanda could promise.

She was trying to get a few things done before the weekend. She made calls and followed up with customers, but the messages kept coming throughout the morning.

Around 10:30, Jacob called Amanda.

"Mom, I am so hot!" Jacob said. Amanda could tell he was outside and he was breathing heavy as he walked. "Dad's working on a tractor, and he's yelling at me because I'm hot and thirsty."

"I'm sure you are," Amanda replied. She was aware that her boss's wife was in the office and easily within earshot.

"I'm walking down the turn row, and I'm going to get in the tractor with Mr. Dave and brother," Jacob explained. "There's air conditioning on that tractor. Will you please call daddy and see if I can come home today. I'm really tired and hot."

"OK, Jacob," Amanda said in a hushed, hurried tone. "I have a lunch break at 11:00 and I can call him then."

"OK, I'm here. I'm getting on the tractor, so just text me what he says," Jacob said.

"OK, I love you. Have a good day," she concluded, and they hung up.

Amanda tried to get busy again quickly. She had to support herself, so she needed to keep this job. She didn't want her boss to think she was lazy or chatting on the phone too much.

When she checked the clock again, it was 10 minutes to 11:00 am. She was going to do one more thing when her cell phone rang.

It was her ex-husband. A call from the governor would have surprised her less. She just didn't talk to the kids' father unless it was absolutely necessary. It was the middle of the day, and he almost never quit work to talk to her. So when she saw his name on the caller ID, alarms signaled in her mind. She tried to quiet them. After all, Jacob had been complaining all morning, maybe his dad was ready to give them up. She was sure it would be short, so she answered the call.

"Hello?" she said.

"Amanda," his voice was urgent, angry and worried all at the same time. "I need you to meet me at the hospital!"

"What?" Amanda quickly asked. She wasn't prepared for

those words. "What is it? What happened?"

"Jacob cut his arm," came the response. "It was cut by the tractor somehow. He may have been run over, but I don't know.

"What do you mean he cut his arm?" Amanda replied. "How did he cut it on the tractor? I was just talking to him a few minutes ago. He was just walking down a turn row."

"Well, just meet me at the hospital," he said, uncertainty and worry in every word, which was very uncharacteristic of the man. "We will go to the hospital in Lake Village. He's going to need stitches. It's bad."

"OK, I'm taking my lunch in 10 minutes, so ..." Amanda said but was cut off before she could finish.

"You have to come now!" he cried.

"Is everything OK?" Amanda asked, hoping for more details.

"Please just hurry up," he said and hung up the phone.

Amanda was left wondering what she should do. She had things to do, a job, plans, but now a strange call to rush to the hospital 40 minutes away, for an injury no one could explain. She stood up wanting to move, but unsure. It seemed unreal, like a dream. Her motherly instincts told her something bad had happened, but her head didn't understand.

The phone was still in her hand, as she turned to her boss' wife.

"That was Jacob's father," she began but was unsure how to explain what she didn't fully understand herself. "He says Jacob cut his arm on the tractor. It's going to need stitches, and he may have been run over by the tractor. They are going to the hospital right now, and he says it's pretty bad so I should meet him at the hospital."

She paused. She stood with an expression of shock, then said, "What should I do?"

"Well, go to the hospital!" cried the boss's wife.

Amanda grabbed her purse and keys. As she ran out the door, she yelled back to her boss's wife, "I'll call you later when I know what happened," and drove away in her car.

Chapter 5
Two Are Broken

Amanda had grown up Pentecostal. Her parents didn't always go to church, but from an early age, Amanda remembered that praying played an important role in her life. No matter what was going on, she always felt better when she prayed. A central principle of her belief is that combining faith with others in united prayer brought the possibilities of miracles. So the first thing Amanda thought to do when she walked out of the building was to get a prayer chain going.

After starting her car, Amanda called her pastor's house. His wife answered.

"Sister Ratley, I need you to pray for Jacob," Amanda said, almost before Sister Ratley could finish saying hello. This motherly woman, wise from years of working with struggling women, could hear in Amanda's voice that she was stressed and worried. "You have to make some phone calls and get people praying for my child."

"What's happened, Amanda?" Sister Ratley said earnestly. "Is Jacob OK?"

"I'm headed north to Lake Village, Arkansas," Amanda said, her chin quivering as she spoke. "That's where they are taking Jacob to the hospital."

Sister Ratley gave an audible gasp.

"Stop by here first, Amanda," Sister Ratley began. "My house is on the way. I will drive you to the hospital. That way you can focus and do whatever you need to do before we get to the hospital. Then, at least you won't be alone."

Amanda agreed and stopped to pick up Sister Ratley. She came out at a brisk walk as soon as Amanda pulled up. Amanda got out and went to the passenger seat. Sister Ratley climbed into the driver's seat and started towards the hospital.

Not knowing what had happened. Amanda didn't want to call a lot of people. But she did call her mother and then her father. Her mother and step-father were working in Florida during the summer, so they weren't going to make it to the hospital very soon, but they would be on the first plane out. Amanda didn't need to ask them to pray for Jacob, they suggested it before Amanda could. Her dad was close by and would be on his way north shortly.

The next call Amanda made was to Whitney - one of her girlfriends. She was the first of the close girlfriends that she thought of and she would help let the others know what was going on. As with her parents, Amanda couldn't explain what had happened or how serious it was because she didn't know. Amanda just said she was on her way to the hospital and please pray for Jacob.

As they drove, Amanda recounted to Sister Ratley the short, cryptic phone call with her ex-husband. She didn't know what had happened, but she just felt like something was severely wrong. He had sounded so different. Sister Ratley continued to encourage Amanda to trust in God and pray.

Amanda got a brief text from Jacob's dad 10 minutes into their drive. All it said was the name of the hospital. Though Amanda was used to driving long distances to get places, this 40-minute drive seemed like it took hours. Her mind raced as she sat and watched the scenery pass by. *How did he get run over? Were they playing around the tractor and fell? They were leveling a field, so was it the big blade that cut him? How did his arm get involved? What other damage did it do? Will he lose his arm?*

The difficulty in getting some bad news and then having time to sit and think about it is not allowing your mind to jump to conclusions. Amanda knew it was bad, or she wouldn't be asked to drive to another state to meet them at the hospital. But there were precious few details beyond that.

'What wasn't he telling me? And Why?' were the questions that kept running through Amanda's head.

Following Sister Ratley's advice, Amanda did pray. Her mind couldn't help but jump to the worst case scenario. What if Jacob was run over by a 15-ton tractor, how could he live through that? So Amanda's pleas to heaven were to spare his life. Tears streamed down Amanda's face as she petitioned God to take anything else but her kids. Take it all, if only Jacob can live, she prayed. If he has to die, let him be alive when I get there.

As they neared the hospital, Amanda saw her ex-husband's truck, and he was standing outside talking on the phone. At that moment, everything just seemed so stupid. Why was she even separated from her child in the first place? Why did they have to go through this? There were a lot of emotions and reasons that caused the divorce, but anything that would separate her from her kids was dumb. This was not what life was supposed to be like.

The SUV had barely stopped rolling when Amanda hopped out and ran to Jacob's father. As she approached, she heard him ask a question.

"So what could we expect if it was broken?" he asked. There was a pause. "Oh, OK. How long would that take to heal? Yeah ... Is it possible that it could keep him from walking?"

Amanda lost it.

She buried her head in his chest and sobbed like a little child. Amanda wanted comfort. She wanted someone to be able to wrap their arms around her and let her know it was going to be OK. Her head knew it was awkward, but her heart was breaking. He didn't console her, though. He only patted her head.

"I need to go, Dusty," Jacob's father said and hung up the phone. Dr. Dusty Smith was not only a doctor, but he was a long-time friend of Amanda and her ex-husband.

"What happened?" Amanda asked as soon as he was off the phone.

"I don't know," he replied, and shook his head as he started to walk back into the hospital.

"Where is Jackson?" Amanda asked before he took two steps.

"He's inside," came the response.

Amanda rushed past her ex-husband, and he called after her, "You can't go back and see Jacob yet. They are doing a few tests."

Amanda heard him, so her full focus turned to her second son. She needed to see him too.

In the waiting room, Amanda saw her 8-year-old son sitting in a chair, clearly in shock. Amanda quickly went to him. Her motherly instincts immediately pushed her personal fears and worries away, because she could see that this son was struggling too. She needed to be the support for him that she was longing for someone to give her.

Amanda knelt down beside Jackson and gave him a hug.

"Jackson, are you OK?" Amanda asked. She brushed a lock of hair from his forehead.

"Mom, I don't think he's going to live," Jackson began, his voice distant and even.

Deep inside, Amanda wanted to yell for someone to tell her what had happened. Why was it a secret that no one would tell her? She wasn't upset with Jackson. She felt like someone that came into a movie half way through, and no one would tell her what was going on.

"What do you mean?" Amanda asked, hoping for a little clarity from her son, who had obviously seen something traumatic.

That was the switch that opened the floodgates.

"We were going to pick him up," Jackson began talking really fast as if the quicker he explained it the sooner Jacob would be saved. "I was beating on the window and yelling at the driver to stop, but he didn't see him. The driver was on the phone. I was watching him, I saw him when he fell. I was looking for him behind the tractor, and the blade pulled over him. It cut his arm. I ran for daddy and he came and pulled him out from under the blade and stood him up. He was bleeding, and I don't think he is going to live. Dad laid him down in the back seat of the truck, and I held him so he wouldn't roll.

"Jacob was awake the whole time," Jackson continued. His eyes darted from side to side like he was watching the scene unfold before his eyes again. Pain and panic coursed through his words. "He was bleeding out of his ear; he was bleeding out of his nose; he was bleeding out of everywhere. Mom, I don't think he is going to live.

"I think Mister Dave ran over him," Jackson concluded and then went silent. His mind shut down to allow the mental wound an opportunity to scab over.

Out of instinct, Amanda wrapped her arms around her son and said, "It's going to be OK."

Amanda felt a flood of new anxiety, despair, and fear about what was going to happen to Jacob. She wanted to run through the halls and find her son. She wanted to yell and scream, but she bottled it up for the sake of the boy in her arms. He needed her right now. The doctors were doing tests on Jacob and parents and visitors weren't allowed to go back anyway. Amanda channeled her emotions and attention on comforting Jackson. She didn't say much but silently prayed for help to get through this together. After a few minutes of silence, Amanda did remind Jackson to pray.

"Pray to God that Jacob will be able to hang on and we will get through this," Amanda said, gently turning Jackson's face to look at hers. "I promise you I'm going to do everything I can to help Jacob. I love you."

"OK, Mom," came the soft, simple response. With the faith of a child, he believed.

While the doctors were taking x-rays, CAT scans, and evaluating Jacob, Amanda anxiously waited for any news. Sister Ratley was busy calling people back home. She called Brother Ratley, Amanda's grandmother, and other devout members of the community, and asked all of them to pray for Jacob. Many of them asked where he was at and how Amanda was doing. Amanda was aware of the phone calls but stayed focused on comforting Jackson and praying for Jacob.

Chapter 6
Under the Blue Sheet

Amanda had been in the waiting room for 10 minutes before the doctors came out to the waiting room to find Jacob's parents. The doctor's expression was grave and worn. Amanda hoped for a little news, but he only said, "You can come back now."

He offered no explanation or expectations for what they would see.

She followed the doctor down the white hallways with large florescent lights, each step full of anticipation about what she would see when they finally got to the room that held Jacob. The first thing she saw was that Jacob's clothes had been cut off and were laying in a heap on the floor. Then she saw Jacob lying on a table with a blue sheet over him. Jacob was pleading to anyone that would listen, "Please give me some water."

Amanda's joy at seeing him alive and talking was slightly checked at the sight of his left arm as she got closer. His arm was laid out and open. There was a long, ugly gash from the top-front side of his shoulder down to his armpit. She could see muscle, fat, and blood.

He's going to lose his arm for sure, Amanda thought to herself.

As hard as living with only one arm would be, she was glad to see that he was talking and that he would probably live through the injury. She turned her attention to Jacob's face. His face looked like he had been rolling in the dirt, which from Jackson's comments, is probably pretty close to

what happened. The doctors were asking Jacob questions
as they moved things. One doctor, picked up Jacob's left leg
slightly and asked, "Does this hurt?"
"Ow! Yes, sir," was his response. "Please don't do that."
"Where does it hurt?" was the follow-up question.
"It hurts around my hips," Jacob replied.
This continued for a few minutes. The doctors would
move or push something and ask Jacob whether it hurt.
Due to the constant back and forth, Amanda didn't say
anything. She gently stroked his head.
At that moment, Jacob's head tilted back towards
Amanda.
"Mom, I can't see you, because I can't see right now, but
I know you are there," Jacob said, his eyes slowly moving
as if to locate her. "I can feel you touching me, and I know
it's not a doctor."
"Baby, I'm here," Amanda said softly, trying to sound
reassuring. She leaned over and gently kissed his forehead.
"You're going to be fine, and I'm not going to leave you.
I'm going to be right here."
"Mom, I don't think I'm going to live," Jacob said with a
slight shake of his head.
"Yes you are," Amanda responded, willing herself to be
optimistic. "Your arm is cut, but we're going to fix it."
"Can you please give me a drink of water?" Jacob asked.
"I'm really thirsty."
Amanda asked the closest nurse if she could just give
him a small drink. The nurse told her no because he is in
shock. He would throw it up. Then the nurse moved on.
All the doctors were looking at x-rays and test results or
poking and prodding. So Amanda grabbed a rag and got it
wet, then she began cleaning Jacob's face. When Jacob felt
the cool, wet cloth on his face, he said, "Mom?"
Amanda just said, "Shhh," while she wiped his face.
As the cloth crossed his lips, Jacob opened his mouth and
started sucking on the rag. Amanda just let him do it. As
he sucked, Amanda looked at one of the x-rays and heard
them say a lung was damaged. Amanda set the cloth down

and approached the doctor that had led them back to the room.

"What happened?" She began. "I need to know what happened. I can see you are doing x-rays on his chest and lungs. What happened?"

The doctor lifted one eyebrow and then walked to the table and pulled back the blue cloth. Amanda gasped reflexively. One hand covered her mouth, the other hand wrapped around her stomach as she staggered back a step to keep herself from fainting.

What she saw were distinct tractor tire marks starting from his right hip, across his abdomen and ending on his left ribs. Amanda knew instantly which tractors they were using because of how perfectly the tread was imprinted on his body. Amanda wanted to stay strong for Jacob. Did he know how bad it was?

"It's really bad, Mom," Jacob said, in a matter-of-fact tone. "It's really bad. I don't think I'm going to live."

Amanda couldn't say much, she said, "Shhh, it's going to be OK." But she didn't trust herself to say much more. The doctor wanted to talk to Jacob's parents outside the room, so he beckoned them to follow him. Amanda reluctantly left Jacob.

In the hall, the doctor explained, "We've called the children's hospital in Little Rock. We are waiting for their Angel One helicopter to transport him. There is nothing more that we can do here. He has a lot of internal bleeding, and his diaphragm has been ruptured. We don't know all of what is wrong. We just know that he has a lot of internal injuries."

He saw the confusion and searching in Amanda's expression, so he continued. "All his organs in his abdomen have been pushed up into his chest cavity. When the tractor ran over him, it smashed everything up. His lung has been punctured, and his pelvic bone has multiple fractures. And of course his left arm is badly lacerated, but luckily the blade didn't cut the main artery."

"Doctor," Amanda said, her eyes electric with the need

to know one thing. "Is he going to make it? I know this is terrible, but is he going to make it?"

"I don't know," came the response. But then the doctor added, "He's losing blood internally. He's losing blood externally. It's going to take the Angel One crew 40 minutes to get here, but they are already in flight. We called for them a while ago. What I need you to do now is to go down to the nurse's station and sign the paperwork, releasing your son to the Angel One team. We will do all we can to keep your son going until they come."

"OK," was all Amanda could say. But before she went to the nurse's station, she went back into the room where her son was. She put her hands on his cheeks and silently prayed. Please God, don't take my son. Take anything I have; my new house, my vehicle, any material thing I have. Take me instead. His life is just starting, and you can't take him right now.

With all her soul, Amanda pleaded that God would spare her son.

Jacob's father suggested that he leave now for Little Rock with Jackson, and Amanda could stay with Jacob and ride with him on the life flight to Little Rock. The doctor and Amanda agreed. So her ex-husband left, Amanda went to sign papers and the doctor returned to Jacob.

Moments later, Amanda saw the nurse's station, but she walked past it. She walked through the double doors to the waiting room. She felt overwhelmed and scared. She knew she needed to sign the papers, but it felt like too much at that moment. She walked through the doors and through the suddenly crowded waiting room. She headed straight for an empty chair in front of her. She fell to her knees in front of the chair and sobbed.

Soon Sister Ratley came over and put an arm around Amanda's shoulders. Then in a soft tone, she said, "Don't give up. Have faith." She paused then added, "You have to believe."

Amanda knew Sister Ratley wasn't scolding her, she was trying to encouraging her, but Amanda was struggling with what she saw and the imminent danger that was threatening her oldest son.

"I'm trying," Amanda cried as she stood up and walked away.

She went about 20 feet and then paused. She took a few deep breaths and focused on her son, and how he needed to be taken care of. She wanted to be strong for him and to make sure he got the care he needed. Mustering what seemed like the last of her composure, she turned to sign the papers that needed to be signed. Crying would have to wait.

When Amanda turned around, she saw more than 20 familiar faces in the waiting room. Her grandmother, cousins, friends, and church members were there. Equal to the gratitude for their support, was her wonder about how they got to the hospital so fast. They must have dropped everything for her and her family. For the first time in hours, Amanda felt a slight smile on her lips as she looked in their loving faces. They didn't come offering advice or telling her what to do. They simply came to show their support. It gave Amanda strength.

At the nurse's station, Amanda went about the mind-numbing task of signing papers. Her son was battling for his life, and she had to autograph a dozen or more papers. Her mind was still with her son, so she just signed and initialed wherever the nurse pointed.

Chapter 7
Angels and Sandals

Just as Amanda finished signing her last page, the Angel One team walked in. Amanda felt like they were real angels, just dressed in jumpsuits. She felt relieved to know they were there, and they would soon be going to Little Rock where pediatric doctors waited to save Jacob's life.

The captain of the angels was a confident man with light brown hair that was turning gray on the sides. His team was efficient and quick with their work. Half the team went to talk to the doctors and get all the particulars about the patient. Others got started setting up the life support systems. They put a tube down Jacob's throat to help with the breathing since his left lung was collapsed. One of the female team members talked with Amanda and got her approval to take Jacob and treat him. She read seven pages of documents with information about "should this happen" and "if this should occur." Amanda didn't try to process everything she said, Amanda just signed the necessary paperwork so they could keep going.

As the team member told her what they would be doing, she mentioned that she would be communicating to her what was going on in the helicopter if things changed. Amanda stopped her.

"I'm going with you, right?" Amanda asked. "You aren't going to leave me behind, are you? It's at least a two-hour drive to Little Rock."

"I'm sorry, ma'am," the crew member said, as she shook her head. Her brown hair pulled back tightly. "We need the space for our crew, and we have a strict dress code, You have to have closed toed shoes. I'm sorry."

The crew member walked away, leaving Amanda feeling helpless once again. How could they take her child without taking her? What if he dies during the flight? She had to ride on that helicopter.

"What size shoe do you wear?" came a female voice, pulling Amanda from her thoughts. It was the nurse that had been going over the paperwork with Amanda earlier.

"I wear a size nine," Amanda replied hopefully. This woman was smaller, but there was a glimmer of hope.

"Oh," the nurse said, her smile fading away. "I wear a size seven, I was going to let you borrow mine if you wanted."

"Can I please?" Amanda said, leaning on the counter that separated them. "I promise to bring them back. Please let me use them."

The nurse took off her shoes, while Amanda removed her leather flip flops. Amanda knew they would not fit, but comfort was the last thing on her mind. She took the shoes and unlaced them as much as possible. She then crammed her feet into the shoes and walked towards the ER room where the Angel One team and doctors were.

She grimaced as she walked, but when she found the crew member she was talking to earlier, she straightened up and announced she was ready to go. The crew member looked at Amanda's feet and shook her head.

"I'm sorry ma'am," he began. "You still can't go with us. What we have to do to him in flight, you aren't going to be able to handle. We have a full crew. We need everyone in our crew to work on him to save his life while we are flying there."

Amanda looked him in the eye and processed what he said. She wanted to hold Jacob and take care of him, but the care he needed, she couldn't give. She realized what this trained emergency paramedic was saying was true. As badly as she wanted to be with him the whole way, she knew she couldn't take the place of one of the crew members who would be able to save Jacob's life.

Amanda took a deep breath and said, "I understand. You

take him and go. I'll be there as soon as I can. Just take him and save him, so when I get there he is alive."

"I understand," said the crew member with a softer tone. "That's why you have to let us take him now."

Amanda went to Jacob while final preparations were being made. Jacob had stopped talking and didn't move much. She could see that his color was draining. Amanda's hope was fading too. She put her hands on his head, stroking his brown hair. She closed her eyes.

As she stood there, the local doctors and nurses gathered around Jacob and grabbed hands. Someone started a simple prayer, asking God to help the doctors, watch over the crew, keep them safe as they flew, and guide the doctors with his care. Amanda was saying her own silent prayer. Please God, fix him. You are the only one that can save him now. Amanda opened her eyes and looked around at the doctors. They had done all they knew to do.

Amanda left as they moved Jacob to the gurney for transportation. She walked out to the waiting room and stood next to her grandmother. The Angel One team walked through the waiting room, one member pumping a bag and another member counting. All were focused on their role, and Amanda felt a little peace knowing Jacob was in good hands. As they exited, Amanda realized she was in no shape to drive two hours. Getting in an accident wouldn't help her family at all. So Amanda looked around and said, "What am I going to do? I can't drive to Little Rock like this. I'm a wreck."

Immediately Rebecca, one of her close friends, stepped forward and said, "I'll take you. Let's go."

Amanda took off the too-small shoes and put her sandals back on. She followed her friend out the door. Amanda didn't have to tell her friend to go fast. She sensed the urgency and flew down the freeway. She maintained a steady speed above 90 miles per hour.

Unfortunately, Rebecca's car wasn't ready for a 130-mile cruise up US-65. On the way, they had to stop for gas. At the gas station, Amanda had to stop her frustration from boiling over. She didn't want to say something mean to her friend that was trying to help her.

Don't be angry, she told herself. *She didn't know she would be driving to Little Rock today. None of us were prepared for this.*

This second long car ride since learning that Jacob was hurt was even more heart-wrenching than the first. Now she had a better understanding of how badly Jacob was hurt, and it was twice as far as the first drive to the hospital. She was aware of how fast her friend was driving, but they couldn't get to Jacob fast enough. Her last view of her oldest child was not encouraging. He had gone from talking to silent; from alert to listless. Would she see her son alive again? The tears flowed almost as fast as they drove. Rebecca couldn't console Amanda.

About an hour into their drive, they crested a hill to find a police officer waiting on the other side. He obviously saw how fast they were going and was quick to flash his lights to pull Rebecca over for speeding. Once they were stopped, the officer came over to the side of the car and leaned over. When he asked, "Is everything OK," he saw Amanda's tear streaked face.

"I'm sorry, Officer," Rebecca began quickly. "But her son was run over by a tractor, and we are rushing to the children's hospital in Little Rock. The life-flight took him from a hospital in Lake Village, and we are desperate to get her there as quick as possible."

"I understand," he said, then tapped the roof of the car. "Please be careful." He walked back to his car, while Rebecca and Amanda drove away.

Despite the two stops, they were able to make it in about an hour and a half. Amanda rushed into the hospital to find out what was going on with her son.

Chapter 8

Little Rock

It was 3:30 pm when Amanda entered Arkansas Children's Hospital. She was immediately escorted to the emergency department where Jacob had been taken by the Angel One team. Rebecca saw Jackson and went to sit with him in the waiting room.

"How is he?" Amanda asked as soon as she saw him laying on a stretcher. "Is he alive?"

"He is alive," said the nearest doctor in light green scrubs. "He was even talking a little bit when he got here. We have already given him a liter of blood, 3.5 liters of plasma and 160 ml of saline solution. He has lost 500 ml of fluids through his chest tubes and catheter. His vital signs are stable, and we are just waiting for word that the operating room is ready so we can take him there."

"They said they would have to add a chest tube in flight and that's why I couldn't go with them," Amanda said, hoping for a little more information. She wasn't understanding everything that was said to her, but as long as they were standing there, she wanted to hear as much as she could in hopes that she would gain a better understanding."

"They did insert another chest tube," the doctor said, nodding his head. "They also put him on full oxygen too, which he has been on since he got here. We are doing all we can to help him stay comfortable until we can get him in the operating room."

Amanda moved to Jacob's head since it seemed to be the only place that she could safely touch. She just tried to stay composed. Amanda wasn't sure if she should dare to hope. She was encouraged that the doctor said he was stable. It almost didn't seem real. It all seemed like a dream. No, not a dream, a nightmare.

As Amanda stood there, one of the nurses looked at her and said, "He had really good manners for being in so much pain."

"Well, I guess we're raising him right," Amanda said with a slight smile. Then she looked back down at Jacob, who seemed to be sleeping. Amanda felt a lump in her throat. "He's a good kid."

The nurse understood Amanda's anxiety. She was like hundreds of other parents that had come to the hospital with their injured child: scared of losing the most precious thing in their life.

The doctor that had spoken to Amanda the first time, calmly but resolutely said, "We will do everything we can to save him."

There was a moment of silence.

"The surgeons will explain a little more just before they take him into surgery," the doctor said before walking away.

Amanda didn't have to wait long. It was only a couple minutes later when the call came that the operating room and doctors were ready. Amanda and Jacob's dad followed the nurses as they pushed Jacob through the halls and to the operating room. The surgeon pulled the parents aside for a brief explanation.

"As you know, your son has been injured badly," he began. "The surgery isn't simple since we can't tell the full extent of his injuries until we go in and take a look."

"We know that the blade that cut his arm missed the main artery by a millimeter," the doctor continued. He looked right at Jacob's dad. "Had the artery been severed, he would have bled to death hours ago, probably before you had gotten to the first hospital. We will try to fix his arm, but we don't want to cut the artery either, so it will be difficult."

"We understand," Amanda responded. "Just fix him. Do what you need to do to save him."

"We don't know exactly how long the surgery will take because we don't know the full extent of his injuries," the doctor continued. "He has a lot of things out of place right now. We won't just be fixing things, we will be doing some exploring because he has so much internal damage. We will call you in the waiting room to give you a report on our progress every 30 minutes. It could be three hours or more before we are done with the surgery, but don't worry if we go longer. We will be thorough and careful."

Amanda's mind grasped the concept, but she was anxious for them to make him better. With some haste, but in a respectful tone, she said, "You don't have to say anything else. Just fix him."

Amanda and her ex-husband went out in the waiting room, not speaking a word to each other.

Amanda quickly learned that this hospital was ready for them in ways she hadn't considered yet. Before Jackson and his dad arrived, the hospital had a counseling service called, Child Life Services, already set up for Jacob, Jackson, and their family. It was a service every patient and family received at the hospital.

Now that Jacob was in surgery, the Child Life Services specialist took the parents into a family counseling room.

"I know you want to be in the waiting room when they call to give you updates, so I wanted to take a moment to make a brief introduction and hopefully start working with Jackson while you wait for information and visit with family," the specialist said. "Child Life Services helps with the psychological and social needs of patients and their families. We are all experts in child development. We try to help the children understand by explaining things to them in a way they will comprehend. When a sibling has witnessed a traumatic incident, we want to help them cope with what they are feeling. We will talk about what's going on with his brother and help prepare Jackson to see his brother again while he is in the hospital. We will also work with Jacob when he comes out of sedation to help him understand where he is and what's going on. Does that make sense?"

Amanda said it did and signed the consent form. At this point, Amanda was pleased that someone was going to help Jackson because she was pretty sure she wouldn't be able to help him. It helped her feel better too that it was a professional that works with kids all the time. It seemed like a ray of sunshine in a rather dark and stormy day.

"Is it OK if we visit with Jackson now?" asked the specialist.

His father thought what they were suggesting was a little excessive.

"Sir, not all wounds are visible," the specialist said, "I don't know how Jackson is doing because I haven't talked to him yet, but I imagine he is pretty upset and anxious about all this. We should never belittle their feelings or ignore them. We are trying to help him cope, and start dealing with what he saw. It may take years before he is fully recovered from what he saw."

Amanda went to Jackson in the waiting room. He had fallen asleep, and the first thing out of his mouth was, "Will Jacob live?"

Amanda's heart nearly broke again, if that was possible. She just said, "They are taking Jacob into surgery. He will be OK. There is a nice lady that wants to visit with you."

Jackson mindlessly obeyed and went into the consulting room with his parents. They went through some introductions, and the specialist said she would play some games and other activities with Jackson for 20 minutes or so. His parents were welcome to stay if they wanted to.

"Jackson, we are going to go in the waiting room to get updates on the surgery," Amanda explained. "It's going to be a long surgery, so you won't miss anything doing things with her in here."

Jackson agreed and stayed with the specialist.

To Amanda's surprise, the waiting room was again full of family and friends. Her pastor and his wife were there. Her grandparents, aunts, uncles and cousins were there. Her best friends were there. As she looked around the room, she felt so much love and strength from everyone. More friends from church were on their way too.

Amanda gave her grandma a hug and prayed with her pastor and his wife. She gave many of the visitors a brief explanation of the current situation: they were just waiting for Jacob to come out of a three-and-a-half-hour surgery and they wouldn't know much more until then. She thanked them for their prayers and concern. She started to sit down but was almost immediately called back for the first of many reports on how the surgery was going.

"We are finished with exploration, and we are going to start repairing lacerated organs," the nurse said. "Your son is in stable condition."

"Thank you for the update," Amanda said. She didn't want to picture the surgery but was happy with the last statement. She hoped that would hold true throughout the operation.

The nurse had also asked that anyone matching Jacob's O+ blood type to please give blood to help replace what was being used for the operation. Several volunteered.

Amanda went to sit down, but when she started to relax, her fears, anxiety and mental images came flooding back, so she decided to stay busy. She called her parents and told them as much as she knew. They said they were headed to the airport and had tickets on an 8:00 pm flight. Then she talked to all the people in the room and told them how much she appreciated them making a long drive up to the hospital for them.

A couple of the visitors were cousins of Jacob and Jackson. When Jackson finished talking with the Child Life Services Specialist, he joined his cousins running around and playing in the outdoor space adjacent to the waiting room. There was a slide, playground, large cave, and bridges over the outdoor stream. Amanda was happy to see Jackson playing. She noticed he would frequently stop and see what his mom and dad were doing. His brother was still on his mind.

Every half hour, the phone would ring, and Amanda would get an update. The most important part was always Jacob's condition. Is he stable? Is he alive? Each affirmative answer to those questions helped raise her hopes a little bit more.

Chapter 9

Operation

Finally, Amanda received the call she had been waiting for - the call to come and talk with the doctor.

The doctor carried with him a piece of paper on a clipboard and a pen. He led Jacob's parents to an operation consulting room. He sat down at a small table with chairs and invited Amanda and her ex-husband to please be seated. Amanda wasn't interested in sitting down but did as he directed. In her mind, she was impatient for him to start. It only took him a moment to gather his thoughts and start, but Amanda nearly blurted out, *Ok, talk! What's happened?* But she held her tongue, and he began.

"First of all, your son is in a drug-induced coma," the doctor began. "He will be on a ventilator for at least a couple days. His body is in shock and in a lot of pain. He is going to need intensive care for at least a week to help him start healing."

Visions of people on life support and hooked up to huge machines played in Amanda's memory from movies and TV shows. Though that was a scary thought, she focused on Jacob starting to heal in a week. She could handle that. She would do anything to help her son get better.

"I will explain what we did in surgery," the doctor said, as he made some marks on his paper. The paper already had two basic bodies printed on it; one facing up and one facing down. He made marks on the paper as he explained the process they went through with Jacob's surgery.

"To fix the five-inch laceration on his left arm, we had to

remove two inches of muscle mass and tissue - one inch from each side of the initial wound site," he said. He drew two little lines on both sides of the original line that indicated where the tractor implement cut his arm. "We needed to get to healthy muscle. Then we closed the wound by attaching muscle and tissue back to the body. We had to be very careful not to hit the artery. We went down the front and up the back side as best we could, but we aren't sure right now how much he will be able to use his arm. We don't know if he has extensive nerve damage or muscle damage. We will be able to tell more about how much he will be able to use his arm as he starts to heal."

When the doctor said, 'starts to heal,' Amanda felt a glimmer of hope spark within her. Jacob would have an arm, and the doctor was already talking about getting better. She was feeling better.

"His internal bleeding increased after he arrived," the doctor continued, drawing two circles where the original chest tubes were inserted on the left and right sides of the rib cage below the nipples. This statement brought Amanda's hope back to reality. "We used 885 milliliters or about 3 units of blood during the surgery in order to maintain fluid levels."

Amanda and her ex-husband both looked like they weren't sure what to do with that information. The doctor explained.

"Think of it as a 12-ounce pop can," he said. "Your bodies have about 12-14 units of blood in them. A 10-year-old boy will have something closer to 8 or 9 units. He lost a lot of blood before he got here, and naturally, he lost more as we operated. It will make more sense as I explain."

He drew a boxy circle, and some squiggly lines that Amanda could tell were supposed to be the intestines. She braced for the rest of the story.

"When the tractor rolled over your son, it rolled over his abdomen," the doctor began again. "Inside your body, you have a diaphragm. It's like a sack where all your intestines are. It helps to keep things in place. It also keeps your digestive system from crowding your lungs and heart. Now imagine you take a sack, fill it with air and then smash it. It pops, right? The pressure from the tractor burst his diaphragm under the right side of his ribs and pushed all his intestines up into his chest. His liver had a laceration that was about 5 millimeters long. His heart and lungs were pushed up and to the right in his chest. One of the lungs collapsed. It was this intense pressure that caused Jacob's eyes to lose sight. We don't know if there was any permanent damage there or not. That will become evident as he heals. There was no need to do surgery on his head at this time."

Amanda's stomach turned. This was hard to listen to, especially since they were describing her son's injuries, not just a CSI investigation. It was personal. She remained focused though.

"We repositioned things and put them in order," the doctor went on, using his hand to motion the downward movement of the intestines. "The blood flow helps to show where the cuts are so we can close them properly. We fixed the liver, any other lacerations, and closed the diaphragm. Lungs are tricky. You can't sew them shut. You have to let them close on their own. That's why we have chest tubes to take the liquid out, so it doesn't go into his lungs. We will have to take x-rays of his lungs periodically to monitor how well they are healing. Once it appears closed, we will be able to remove the chest tubes."

Amanda felt herself exhale as she listened to the ending. But it wasn't the ending.

"He also has a couple of transverse spinal fractures, but they didn't require surgery to fix them," the doctor continued, drawing fracture lines on the spine. As he continued he drew fracture lines on the waist portion of the child image. He said, "The tractor tire also broke his pelvic bone in several places. He can't withstand another surgery right now, so we have put everything in order as best we could, hoping it will heal properly since he is young and his bones are still growing. If it doesn't heal properly, he will need to have another surgery to insert a metal plate that will keep everything in place. That would take place on Monday, if needed."

Another surgery? Amanda thought. *Let's get through this one first.*

"When can I see him and talk to him?" Amanda asked when the doctor was finished.

"Right now, they are moving him to the Pediatric Intensive Care Unit, or PICU," responded the doctor. "We can start heading that way, but you will not be able to talk with him for a week.

"I must caution you, though," the doctor said as they stood to go to the PICU, "He is by no means through this ordeal. We will have to monitor him constantly. We will watch his progress by the hour for the first couple days, and then we will see what needs to happen."

They walked through the bright white halls of the hospital to the Pediatric Intensive Care Unit on the third floor. Amanda wanted to run to see her son, but she was worried about how he would look when she got there.

Chapter 10
Tubes And Machines

As they entered the double doors into the PICU area, Amanda saw that there were sets of nurses' stations with five or six nurses performing various tasks at each one. There were more than a dozen rooms with clear glass doors that stretched down the unit across from the nurses' station. Each room had a sliding glass door and curtains that could be closed to give a patient some privacy. Amanda could see that this configuration made it easier for each of the patients to be observed and quickly reached if an alarm were to sound. She could see that 12 nurses were on duty at all times. She could hear beeps from monitors and breathing machines. It was all reassuring and unnerving at the same time.

The doctor led Amanda and Jacob's dad to a room with a boy who had about 10 to 15 tubes and sensors on him. It looked like Jacob, but his body was swollen. Even his fingers were swollen. The trauma of the tractor rolling on him, and then a long, difficult surgery had caused his skin to balloon. Amanda was stunned. She stepped closer to his bed. She wanted to reach down and embrace him but knew she couldn't. Instead, she bent over to kiss his head. His hair had the familiar smell of her son. It was him.

Jacob had two tubes held in place by a white apparatus that looked like the bottom half of a football helmet. There was one tube in his nose and one in his mouth, both secured by strips of tape. They connected to a plastic piece with a loop on both sides where the fabric was connected and wrapped around the back of his head holding it all in place.

A light blue gown with a navy blue pattern covered his body. Both arms were propped up with pillows. There were IVs in his right hand and a blood flow sensor on his left thumb, half a dozen other tubes were on and around his arms, but Amanda didn't know what they were for. His arms had tan, padded cuffs on them with nylon cords attaching them to the bed.

Amanda could see how the bed was positioned to allow Jacob's pelvic bone to heal. His legs were covered with a sheet. She could see that his legs were spread with his right foot angled in slightly more than the left. There were blood pressure cuffs and circulation cuffs on his legs to help with the circulation in his legs.

 Amanda fought the tears that threatened to pour. She wanted to be strong. She wanted to hope for the best, but it was obvious that the machines were breathing for him. It was obvious that he was in bad shape. What more could he go through and live? Would he endure what had happened and recover?

"As you can see, the ventilator is helping him breathe," the doctor explained. "The nurses will monitor his blood pressure, heart rate, breathing and all other vital signs around the clock. There will also be specialists that will come in and review his records and make recommendations according to what they see."

Amanda nodded, but never looked away from Jacob.

"I'm aware that you have family and friends here," the doctor continued. "I'm afraid we can't have all of them come up at the same time, and we have strict rules about who may come into the PICU. Only close family are allowed, and they can only come with either of you - one or two at a time. It's to keep the whole unit from getting too congested. For that same reason, we don't allow lots of bags, toys, balloons or other things like that. We have a locker that you may use.

"There is a chair here that you may use," the doctor continued as he motioned toward the chair. "But you may not sleep through the night here. We suggest that you use the family room on the second floor to get some rest at night if you don't want to find a hotel room."

"I'm not leaving my son in this condition," Amanda said resolutely.

"We hear that a lot," said the doctor, not at all offended by her tone. "That's why we have a guest shower that you may use if you need to. We aren't a 5-star hotel, but we try to be as accommodating as possible."

"Thank you," Amanda said in a softer tone. She still wouldn't look away from her son.

"If you need anything or want to talk, Child Life Services will gladly help you any way they can," the doctor said, as he reached out to shake Jacob's father's hand and then Amanda's. "They do a fantastic job with the families as they transition out of the hospital and back into life. They are a good resource for you."

Amanda thanked him again, and he left.

There was an awkward silence between Amanda and her ex-husband. Both were trying to assess what to do now. Jacob's dad eventually said he would walk back to the waiting room and let everyone know that only immediate family could see Jacob right now. Amanda only nodded once and sat down.

Amanda sat in the rocking chair next to Jacob's bed. Since 11:00 am that morning, she had endured dozens of surprises and unexpected problems. It had been a frantic mess ever since she hung up the phone more than seven hours ago. For the first time since that fateful call, she wasn't bracing for the next big revelation or shocking turn of events. In her mind, she relived the day and teetered precariously between relief, exhaustion, and fear. She wanted to reach out and hold Jacob's hand but feared it would explode because of how swollen it was. She talked to him a little, unsure how much good it did since he was in a coma. It helped her a little.

After about 20 minutes, Amanda got a text from her friend Rebecca letting her know that Jackson and a couple others wanted to say goodbye. Though she hadn't taken a direct route to the PICU from the waiting room, it was pretty easy to find with the signage. She learned it quickly since she knew she would be there for a while.

Amanda closed her eyes. Mentally it made sense. Jackson was her son too, and Jacob would probably not change much in the five or ten minutes it took to say goodbye. Emotionally, she felt like a tree that had been hacked into by an ax repeatedly; one gust of wind or blow of the ax would bring her down. She did go, hoping that it would somehow strengthen her rather than make her weaker.

She was once again surprised by how many people were there in the waiting room. Not only did Jackson come up to give her a long hug, but Ally did as well. Amanda's paternal grandma had picked up Ally from daycare and would take care of her for Amanda as long as she needed. This statement helped Amanda realize how consumed she had been. She had all but forgotten her daughter in all the chaos. She had only remembered Jackson a couple of times in the hours since the incident. How was she going to manage it all? Amanda embraced this loving gray-haired woman they called Granny with tears in her eyes. The look on Amanda's face brought words of comfort and solace from the tender grandmother.

"There, there, dear," Granny began as she patted Amanda on the back while they embraced. "Life always looks scariest in the moment of darkness. Just hold on and morning will come again."

"Thank you," Amanda said, wiping away her tears. "I will try to not lose hope. It just seems like a lot to take in right now."

"Of course it is, but you aren't alone," Granny said. "There are a lot of us anxious to help you, so don't try to do everything on your own. Let us help."

Amanda smiled and tried her best to be positive while the rest of the family and friends came up to say goodbye. One by one they expressed their willingness to do anything that she needed, but Amanda could only say, "thank you." Rebecca volunteered to go back to Amanda's house and get a change of clothes and toiletries so she could stay without interruption. Amanda asked for a few changes of clothes as she wasn't sure how many days or weeks she would be there.

It was about 8:00 pm before all the friends and family had stopped coming up to see Jacob and Amanda. Jacob's father said he was going to take Jackson and get a hotel room. And so Amanda took up her silent vigil of watching over her oldest son. She sat in silence, aside from the ever-present machine noise, not able to process anything new. She felt emotionally numb.

Before she knew it an hour and a half passed. Not wanting to leave, she found herself falling asleep in the chair next to Jacob's bed. The exertion and excitement of the day had overpowered her body, and she needed to close her eyes.

Just after midnight, Amanda woke up to a nurse gently calling her name.

"Ma'am," the nurse began when Amanda was finally making eye contact. "There is a couple downstairs, a Michael and Penny. They want to see you. I think they said they are your parents."

"Oh," was all Amanda could say as she continued to try and make sense of what the nurse was saying. Amanda looked at her watch and noticed the time. Yes, it was about the time her parents said they would be arriving. She looked at Jacob. He was in the exact position he was in before with little variation in condition. Amanda decided the exercise and break might be good.

"Ma'am," the nurse began again as Amanda was getting up. "We will watch over your son very closely. If you would like to get some better rest in the patients' family room, you will probably be more comfortable and get better sleep there. You have to take care of yourself too."

"Thank you," Amanda said a weak smile on her face due to the genuine concern the nurse showed. "I will bring my parent's up, and then I may go back down to get some sleep."

Amanda went down to the waiting room. As she exited the elevator and walked to the waiting room, Amanda saw her parents. They were sitting on a green vinyl couch, their small travel bags on the floor next to them. They got up immediately when Amanda walked off the elevator.

Amanda walked up and hugged her mom.

"How is he?" Penny asked.

"Do you want to go see him?" Amanda asked.

Penny and Michael hesitated but finally agreed. Amanda led them back to the PICU and then to Jacob's room. Penny and Michael walked with trepidation. They were anxious and yet reluctant to see Jacob in his current state.

The first thing Amanda's mother noticed was towers of machines around the bed. Then she followed the tubes and hoses to Jacob's swollen body. It was hard to believe what she was looking at. Was this really the young boy that had been growing up so quickly when they left for Florida? Was this the little boy that had the cute little smile with round cheeks and loving eyes?

Penny put an arm around Amanda and a hand over her mouth. A tear escaped Penny's eyes, and she quickly tried to compose herself. She wanted to be strong for Amanda, and keep her hopes up.

Amanda embraced Penny and cried. She knew this must be shocking for Penny to see her grandson like this, but Amanda needed to lean on her mother right then.

It was a full five minutes of silence as Amanda sobbed on Penny's shoulder. Her mom didn't speak, she didn't know what to say, but she held her daughter and let her cry. Michael's heart broke for his stepdaughter and Jacob. They didn't rush Amanda. They just said silent prayers, not knowing what else they could do.

Eventually, Amanda let go of her mother and began explaining what she knew of the situation. She gave as much information as she could remember about the tractor incident, the first hospital, the life flight, and the surgery.

Mother and daughter stood in silence for a few minutes before a nurse came in to check Jacob's IV bags. Penny turned her attention to Amanda and asked how she was doing. They talked for a while and then went back to the waiting room. Michael tried his best to encourage Amanda not to lose hope.

His words were shaky though, and Amanda knew he saw the seriousness of the situation just as she had.

Due to the late hour and all the travel, Penny and Michael went to a hotel room shortly before 1:00 am. Amanda got a pillow and sheet from the nurses and tried to sleep in the family room. It was fitful sleep since her mind continued to go back to her 10-year-old son lying in a coma in an out-of-state hospital, and she was laying on a stiff couch.

Chapter 11
A Cross Road

By 6:00 am, she was back in the room with Jacob. She wasn't there long before a nurse came in to run vitals. The nurse noted that Jacob was running a temperature of 101.5. She left to get orders from the doctor to apply Tylenol to reduce his temperature. Jacob's elevated temperature also elevated Amanda's heart rate, but the nurse remained calm. Amanda tried to follow suit. The nurse returned shortly with the Tylenol as well as a lubrication that she put on Jacob's eyes which looked red and swollen. When Amanda asked what it was for, the nurse explained that the gel helped to keep moisture on the eye.

"Normally we blink, and that hydrates our eyes," the nurse said. "Since Jacob is sedated, he isn't blinking, so we put this gel on to keep the eyes moist."

The nurse left Amanda alone with her son for 20 minutes.

As she sat, her mind now went to the life she had put on hold less than 24 hours before. Question after question flooded her mind. *How long will we be in this hospital? If he gets out of here - no, when he gets out of here - what shape will he be in? Will he get out of here? Yes, he will. When he does will he be blind? Will he be able to walk? Will he have the use of his arm again?*

Amanda looked at the machines and started wondering: *How much is this going to cost? It will all be worth it if he lives, but how am I going to pay for this? Am I going to even have a job when this is done? What will I do if I lose my job?*

Her anxiety rose.

I can't keep a job while I have to take care of my son all day, she said to herself. *I can't leave him with a babysitter. What about the other kids? How will they handle all this? Will Jackson recover from seeing his brother run over by a tractor?*

Amanda bowed her head and again prayed that God would help them make it through.

The nurse came back in at 6:30 am, and Jacob's fever was now 99.3. Amanda felt a little more reassurance with Jacob's fever already going down. She hoped it wasn't a sign of infection. The nurse didn't think that was the case. Amanda continued her silent watch until about 7:00 am when her ex-husband walked in with his girlfriend. They had taken Jackson back to Child Life Services before coming up. Amanda was lost in her own thoughts, and her ex-husband wasn't going to help her much. She said she would go take a shower and see if she could find something to eat.

Amanda needed clothes before she could take a shower, so she called Rebecca to see if she would be able to bring up clothes. Rebecca said she was only about 10 minutes away from the hospital with Amanda's things. Amanda went to the front lobby to meet Rebecca.

"I thought you would prefer comfort over style while you are here, so I grabbed some jeans and shirts," Rebecca said, after a quick hug and hello. She opened the bag to show Amanda what she brought. "I hope that's OK."

"That will be fine," Amanda replied and gave her friend another hug. "How did you get it so quickly? I didn't expect you up here so soon."

"Your grandmother let me in," Rebecca said. "We arranged to get things before we left the hospital last night."

"Oh," Amanda said, surprised how quickly her friends and family were acting to help her. She lifted her bag of clothes slightly and said, "Thank you for bringing this to me."

"Of course," Rebecca said with a wave of her hand. "I wanted to come up and see how you are doing."

"Treading water," Amanda said and used her hand to show the water rising above her head.

"Is there anything I can do to help," Rebecca implored, searching for anything to alleviate her friend's load.

Amanda thought about it and realized she didn't know if anyone could help.

"No, I think we just have to wait right now," Amanda said. "Just keep praying for us."

After Rebecca left, Amanda went back up to the family room by the PICU and cleaned up and changed clothes.

***

While Amanda was cleaning up, Jackson was in meeting with another member of the Child Life Services team. Jackson wasn't sure what they would do this time. The evening before he just learned about what Child Life Services does and then got to play a game with the specialist. He wanted to ask this specialist if she knew how Jacob was doing.

"Hello Jackson, my name is Deirdre," she began once they both were seated. "I want to help you understand what's going on with your brother. So tell me what you know already, and we will start with that."

Jackson related the incident much like he had to his mother. He began to cry again and added, "Before the tractor completely stopped, I jumped out and ran to get dad. He didn't understand what I was screaming about and ran back with me. Dad picked up Jacob, but he couldn't stand, and his arm was bleeding. Jacob had blood coming out of his mouth, nose, and ears. When Dad went to get the truck, I prayed for my brother. I had to hold him on the backseat as we drove to the closest hospital.

"I was told to keep him from sliding off," Jackson continued. Jackson would kind of turn his body and make movements that showed he was reliving the event in his mind. "I got blood on my shirt, but I was just crying and praying he would be okay. I know they couldn't fix him all the way at the first hospital, so they had to fly him in a helicopter to this hospital. All I know is he went into surgery last night, and he's alive. I think."

"Yes, he is alive," Deirdre said. Her own heart had

broken to see this eight-year-old boy relive the experience again, but she knew it could be helpful. "Thank you, you did a good thing by getting your dad and helping out. I see a lot of children here that are worried about their brothers or sisters that have to come to the hospital. You may feel scared or worried, but we want to help you and Jacob feel better."

Deirdre smiled at Jackson, and he wiped away a tear.

"Do you want to see a picture of your brother and his room?" Deirdre asked.

"Yeah," Jackson replied. His eyes brightening at the prospect of seeing his brother.

"You can stop me at any point and ask me questions. You don't have to wait," she explained to Jackson.

Deirdre pulled out a hand-full of pictures. The first picture was of a room with glass walls and doors. It had a bunch of machines around a bed. There was a counter in the foreground.

"Do you know where this is?" Deirdre asked. After he had said no, she said, "This is your brother's room. He's in the Pediatric Intensive Care Unit. That just means it's the place where they take care of kids that need to be watched very closely. He has his own nurse that is taking care of him at all times. There are a lot of machines here so I will tell you what they are and how they work."

Deirdre put that picture down and exposed the second picture. It was a close-up shot of a screen with numbers and lines on it.

"What does that look like?" Deirdre asked with a smile; encouraging Jackson to participate.

"It looks kind of like a computer screen," he said, looking a little closer.

"You're right," Deirdre said. "It's a monitor that shows us how the heart is beating. All the kids in the PICU have one of these machines. It tells us the heart rate, the blood pressure, and things like that. It tells us how Jacob is doing on the inside. It tells us if something is going wrong inside before you could see the problem on the outside."

Jackson nodded.

Then Deirdre followed a similar process with the IV pumps, ventilator, and other machines. She explained their functions in simple terms that Jackson could understand and process easily. Then she showed the first picture of Jacob in his bed. Jackson was surprised at first but didn't shy away.

"Your brother has a c-collar on his neck," Deirdre explained. "Any time a child comes in after any fall or collision, especially if he's asleep like your brother, we put on this collar so we can protect their neck. Jacob can't tell us if his neck hurts, so we use the collar to protect his neck so we don't cause any more harm.

"Do you see those tubes on Jacob's arms?" Deirdre asked. Jackson nodded. "Those tubes make it so we can give medicine to Jacob.

"How does your mom give you medicine at home?" Deirdre asked.

"I swallow it," Jackson replied.

"That's right," Deirdre said. "Jacob can't swallow, so we have to use the tubes that go right into his blood system to give him fluids and medicine. You can see that he is just laying there. That's because he is sleeping. We have given him medicine to help him sleep for a while so that his body can heal without him moving a lot. Jacob isn't in pain right now, which is a good thing."

Deirdre put down the picture of Jacob in bed and revealed the last picture. It showed just Jacob's covered shoulders and head.

"This is what your brother looks like right now," Deirdre said, then let Jackson look at it for a moment without saying anything. She wanted to see if he would have questions.

"Why is he so fat?" Jackson asked. He had leaned closer to the picture as if to make sure it was his brother.

"He looks a little different, doesn't he?" Deirdre responded. "During the surgery, they gave him fluids and blood to help him replenish the blood he lost. His body will absorb the fluid, and he will look more normal in a couple days.

"What are those tubes in his nose?" Jackson asked, wrinkling his own nose as he asked.

"The larger white tube goes to the ventilator, and it helps Jacob breath," Deirdre explained. "The clear tube in his nose actually goes down into his stomach and take away any extra air or fluids there. When we get too much air in our stomach, we get nauseous. Do you know what that mean?"

"Isn't that when you need to throw up?" Jackson replied.

"That's right," Deirdre said. "We don't want that to happen, so we use that tube to keep Jacob from feeling like he needs to throw up.

"What's the shiny stuff on his eyes?" Jackson asked, pointing to Jacob's closed eyes in the picture.

"We blink our eyes to keep our eyes moist," Deirdre explained. "Right now, Jacob can't blink because he is in a deep sleep. So the nurses put some Vaseline solution on his eyes to help keep them moist."

Jackson stopped asking questions and just looked at Jacob.

"Do you want to go see Jacob today?" Deirdre asked. She immediately added, "You don't have to see him, but it's alright if you do. Either way is fine."

"Yes," Jackson said with only a slight hesitation. "I want to see brother."

"OK, your dad is up there now," Deirdre said. "Let's go see your brother."

Jackson and Deirdre walked slowly down the hall toward the PICU room. Deirdre let Jackson dictate the pace. They went through the double doors and turned left and walked past one room. When Jackson saw his dad, he knew he was about to see Jacob. Jackson walked in to find that things were pretty much the same as he had seen in the pictures. He recognized what was there, and Deirdre had told him about the noises he was experiencing now.

Jackson stood next to his brother's bed and stared. Jacob was swollen, but not quite as bad as in the picture. He touched his hand and felt it was warm. Jackson looked at his dad and Deirdre for any other clues, and they looked back at him without fear or panic on their faces. Jackson assumed that meant Jacob was doing alright.

Jackson felt much better.

***

After Amanda was cleaned up and in a fresh set of clothes, she realized she hadn't eaten since breakfast the previous day, so she went to the cafeteria in the hospital. Due to her Celiac disease and not wanting to search all the labels for wheat ingredients, she decided to just eat a banana and get a cup of coffee. She walked back to the dining area, which was surprisingly quiet for a weekend morning. The view from the dining area overlooked the Little Rock Capital building. She stood at the window facing north, but she wasn't really looking.

"Why is this happening, God?" she prayed silently. "We were just getting our life in order after the divorce? I just got that house. Jacob was going to start fifth grade. I was going to take my test and life was finally looking up for us. Why did this have to happen?"

Amanda fidgeted with her jewelry like she normally did when lost in thought. Like a strike of lightning, Amanda had a surge of peace come into her heart when she grabbed her cross necklace. It wasn't a voice, but it was like her thoughts were being led. She didn't struggle because she knew it was an answer to her prayer.

She saw the extra messages from Jacob before the incident. She saw the people that were there supporting her from almost the instant she learned about what happened to Jacob. She remembered the encouraging note from Sister Ratley. Amanda had a clear view of the vision she had experienced a year before. It was as if the Lord was telling her, "I am in control. It will be OK. I will take care of your family. You have to trust me. I put these things and more in your path to help you get through this. I will not leave you."

"I understand Lord," Amanda said in her mind. She was full of peace and gratitude for this experience. "I'm sorry for doubting you. Thank you for helping me see this."

Amanda sat in silent reflection. Tears came down her face.

She remembered from her dream how Christ had absorbed the destruction and protected her kids. Jacob was obviously not whole right now, and she didn't get any guarantee that he would be whole, but she knew God was in charge and was taking care of them. For the first time in almost 24 hours, she was able to forget the fear and worries. She clung to the peace for as long as she could.

Amanda found Jackson in the waiting room. He had recently come back from visiting Jacob. They went to the third floor where there was a play area called Camp Wannaplay. It had an outdoor playground as well as indoor space with a Wii, coloring stations, a foosball table and other games. Child Life Services had suggested it to Amanda as a good place to unwind with Jackson. They spent the next hour or so playing games, talking about what Jackson got to do after they left the hospital, and anything else she could think of that didn't relate to Jacob and the tractor incident. It was a good break for Amanda and Jackson.

Jackson didn't mention the visit with Jacob, not because he didn't want to, but it seemed like his mom was focusing on other things. Maybe it was hard for her to talk about Jacob, or she needed a break from thinking about that. He felt more confident things would be OK, after seeing Jacob. He didn't feel like he had to talk about Jacob to learn more about what was going on. Mother and son were able to rest their minds on their injured son and brother in a coma down the hall.

Chapter 12
Sleeping Through Tests

Around 9:30 am, Amanda saw Jacob's father and his girlfriend walk out of the elevator. Amanda quietly walked toward the elevator and back up to the PICU. When she arrived at Jacob's room, she saw a team of doctors around his bed. At first, Amanda was a little concerned, but she noticed that there wasn't a lot of urgency in their body language and speech. When she got closer, the doctor closest to her son, who was speaking to the group, turned his attention to Amanda.

"Are you the boy's mother?" he asked, now that she had reached the group. All the other doctors turned and smiled.

"I am," Amanda replied. "What's happened?"

"Well, not much has happened since you last saw him," the doctor said, looking back at the clipboard in his hands. "I am the lead neurologist on duty, and these men and women are doctors and residents. We were going over the results of the brain scans and were discussing your son's condition."

"And what have you concluded?" Amanda asked, steeling herself for the worst. "What kind of long-lasting damage are we going to face?"

"I'm afraid it's far too early to know the outcome yet," the neurologist replied with a slight shake of his head. "We won't know that until he wakes up, and even then we will have to see how he recovers. But these initial results are positive. We will be monitoring him daily."

Amanda nodded her head and looked down.

The doctors talked amongst themselves for a few more minutes, and then left Jacob's room and went to see another patient. Many shook Amanda's hand and wished her a good day. They all seemed pleasant and happy.

This scene played out during the rest of the day, one team after another came through and looked at different test results, vital signs, oxygen levels, blood levels. They took x-rays and discussed the results among themselves and with Amanda. There were cardiologists, pediatricians, urologists, oncologists, and other teams of five to seven doctors and students coming to Jacob's bedside. If it wasn't doctors coming through, the nurses were frequently checking on him.

When there was a moment of quiet, between the dozens of medical personnel coming in, Amanda would move to the edge of her seat and lean over the side of Jacob's bed. She would talk to Jacob.

"I don't know if you can hear me," Amanda would say. "But I just want you to know we are doing everything we can to take care of you and get you back to good. I'm not sure how we are going to get through this, but we will. I'm praying that God will help us get through this."

Amanda stroked his head. It was the only place she felt she could touch without messing up any cords or tubes.

"Just don't quit, Jacob," Amanda said, her voice more fervent and pleading. "I don't know how you are feeling or what you are going through, but I want you to stay with me. We are going to get through this together."

Amanda stayed with Jacob as long as she could. It was around 11:30 pm when a nurse asked if she needed a pillow and blanket to take down to the family room. Amanda could take the hint. While the chair wasn't very comfortable, she wished she could just stay close to Jacob. With one last kiss goodbye, Amanda promised Jacob she would be back in a few hours.

The nurse noticed Amanda's longing to stay close to her son.

"Don't worry ma'am," she said with a smile. "We will

page you if anything changes. But he's been steady all day. I'm sure he will be fine."

"I know," Amanda said, grabbing her purse and then heading out of the room. "It's just a couple minutes away to the waiting room, but I just worry about something happening while I'm away and I can't get to him in time."

Amanda didn't sleep very well that night either. Stiff couches were not meant for a comfortable night's sleep. By 6 am, she was back at Jacob's side, and there was no change. She felt a little irritated that she worried so much, and couldn't sleep better. She wouldn't take any time for granted.

Sunday rolled on much like Saturday had. Teams of doctors came and went; checking, looking, nodding, discussing. They would explain things to Amanda, which she was grateful for, but they never gave her a simple answer to her burning question: What would his body be like when he woke up? What lasting effects would he have to deal with? It was too soon to tell, or some variation of that was all they would say.

At 9:00 am, Amanda got a phone call from her cousin, Tiffany. Tiffany was studying at LSU in Baton Rouge. She had taken some time away from her studies to create a CaringBridge account for Jacob. Amanda wasn't familiar with CaringBridge. Tiffany explained that it was a non-profit site that allowed family and friends to get updates on how Jacob was doing and even make donations to help with costs. It was a little more private than all the other social media sites. And other users could share encouraging messages with the patient and his family. Amanda looked at the site for a while between doctor checks. It was interesting how many strangers had already posted a prayer for Jacob or an encouraging message for his parents.

Around 11 am, two nurses came and started unhooking a couple of the monitors. Amanda was a little unnerved by this, but they saw her panic and calmly explained.

"We are just going to take him down to get an MRI," said the radiology tech with a smile. "We need to see how things are healing inside. The MRI machine is too big to bring in here."

"Oh, sure," Amanda said, understanding now what was going on. "Should I just stay here?"

"Yes, we will bring him back shortly," was the reply, and they wheeled Jacob away.

As promised, they did bring him back in about 20 minutes. While they were gone, a nurse had come in with a packet of papers for Amanda to fill out and sign. There was also a checklist of things she needed to go over or do. Amanda was pleased with the order and preparedness of this hospital.

At noon, she was greeted by a friendly woman from Child Life Services. Her name was Esther. She had brown hair, brown eyes, and a warm smile. She asked Amanda to follow her to her office so she could go over a few things. Jacob's father was at the door. Amanda figured this would be a good time to stretch her legs and let him sit with Jacob.

Chapter 13
Child Life Services

Esther led Amanda into her office a few floors below the PICU. Esther had pictures of her kids on the desk next to her computer. In Esther's hand was a folder with Jackson's name on it. It still amazed Amanda how completely she was focused on Jacob. She hadn't forgotten about Jackson, but she had devoted so much time to Jacob that she was suddenly concerned that Jackson was not doing well. She had talked to him yesterday, but after such a traumatic experience a lot could have changed in 24 hours.

"Ms. Brown, I'm sorry that your son is in the PICU," Esther began. "We know that this is a very difficult time for you and your family. I hope by now that you believe your son is in capable hands here. We will do all we can to make sure he has the best recovery possible."

"Yes, I have been very pleased with the staff and care of Jacob," Amanda replied.

"Good," Esther said. "I hope that continues."

"My focus here at the hospital is to help families, but specifically children, get through traumatic experiences like yours," she continued as she opened the file. "As you are aware, Jackson witnessed a devastating incident that nearly took the life of his brother. He was in shock when he came in here the first day, and we try to help him find ways of expressing his emotions so that he can start to recover. Part of the recovery process was seeing his brother for the first time."

"Really?" Amanda asked. "When did you do that? I would think that Jackson would be horrified to see Jacob in a coma."

"Well to spring it on him all of a sudden, it probably would," Esther replied. She was unphased by the comment because she had heard similar comments many times over the years she worked at the hospital. "We took pictures of Jacob after surgery. We asked Jackson if he wanted to see a picture of Jacob in his room in the PICU. He said he did, and we showed him the picture and discussed the machines and how Jacob was sleeping now, but the doctors and nurses were taking good care of him. He was surprised to see his brother like this, but it's easier to see it in a picture before he sees it in person."

Amanda nodded. She was glad they knew what they were doing. She was sure that Ally would have to wait to see Jacob until he was talking and didn't have so many tubes and wires stuck to him.

"You must remember that when he last saw his brother, he was trying to keep him from sliding off the back seat of his dad's pickup with blood coming out of his ears, nose and mouth, and a left arm that was nearly cut off. These pictures of Jacob in his hospital bed are hard to take, but it's a better image than the mental images that were playing in his mind the first 24 hours."

That was true. Amanda hadn't thought about it that way, but the mental image of her 8-year-old son holding his big brother on the seat made Amanda's heart break all over again. *Why did they have to go through this,* she thought to herself.

"Jackson is a resilient boy," Esther continued, breaking into Amanda's reflections. "But the mind can be fragile at times like this, so it's really important that we pay attention to the way Jackson acts. If his sleeping, eating or moods change a lot, we need to talk with him and see how he's doing mentally. It may not happen for a couple of weeks, so just know that until Jacob is home and life resumes close to normal, Jackson could be in danger of struggling too."

"I understand," Amanda said. She hoped she would know what to do if that happened.

I'm not sure I won't crack if this keeps going for a couple of weeks, she thought to herself. *I could use someone to talk to.*

"How are you handling things, Ms. Brown" Esther asked, again breaking Amanda's inner dialog.

"Well, I don't know if anything can prepare you to see your son in the hospital like this," Amanda said, consciously trying to control her emotions. "There are a lot of worries and fears on my mind right now, but I just want to be strong for my son."

A rogue tear fell from Amanda's eyes.

"I can't leave him for long because I'm worried I won't see him alive again," Amanda went on. "I know the staff is capable, and I trust they are doing all they can, but I just pray that God will let him live. I don't know how we will make it financially after this. I haven't a clue what a helicopter and a team of doctors costs, but I'm sure it's not cheap. But I don't care, as long as my son get better. We'll find a way to make it through."

Amanda was silent. Esther waited quietly and let Amanda think.

"The top priority of everyone here is to get Jacob better," Esther said when it looked like Amanda was more composed. "We will do everything we can to help you as well. We don't want to break you in the process of saving your son. We are here for you as well as your boys. No one ever counts on these things happening, so we work with insurance companies, make payment plans, and so forth. We will work with you."

Esther looked Amanda in the eyes and smiled, "But for now, we need to talk a little bit more about Jackson and how we can help him."

They spent another 35 minutes talking about what to look for and how to help Jackson cope. Esther had confirmed what Amanda had felt, she shouldn't try to force Jackson to relive the incident. She shouldn't talk about blaming people for what happened; leave it for grownups to discuss. Jackson needed positive reinforcement, without lying to him, about the situation and help him think about other things when he is struggling.

Chapter 14
Learning to Breath

After Amanda returned to Jacob's bedside, the orthopedic surgeon came to his room and told Amanda that after looking at the latest x-rays they could see that the pelvic bone wasn't going to heal properly.

"What's wrong?" Amanda asked. "What can you do about it?"

"The head surgeon may have mentioned that we might have to go in and fix his pelvic bone if it didn't heal properly," the doctor replied. "You had a lot going on that day. We were worried that Jacob wouldn't react well to more surgery than we were already doing, so we wanted to see how it would heal if we just sat him up."

Amanda nodded her head. She remembered that comment being made, but the thought of another surgery now seemed inconceivable.

"But if we wait much longer, the bones will try to heal as they are," he continued. Then he picked up his clipboard and drew part of a body and pointed as he talked. "So what we will do is make an incision here and attach a 12-inch metal plate here on the right side of his pelvic bone. It will hold the bones in place so they will grow back together properly. Over the next four to six weeks, he will need to keep the weight off of his pelvic bone. Walking and standing are out of the question for four weeks at least. But this plate will help him heal properly and get back to walking."

"OK," Amanda said. She trusted the doctors here, but

the thought of another surgery and a metal plate on his pelvic bone was a little scary right now. *He makes it sound so simple, she thought to herself. In his mind, it is simple because they probably do it frequently.*

"What day would this need to happen?" Amanda asked as she tried to remember if the head surgeon had already told her that or not.

"We will take him in to operate tomorrow morning at 7:00 am," he said, putting his clipboard down by his side. "We should have him in and out in an hour. Do you have any other questions?"

Amanda and the doctor discussed the procedure a little more, and he left.

Amanda remembered that it was Sunday, and how much she looked forward to Sunday's before. She wasn't home to cook, but she wanted Jacob to know she was still there. Amanda picked up her Bible and started reading in Matthew. She thought, *At least he can hear my voice. And there might be some added comfort in here for me too.*

She finished reading when another team of doctors came to check on Jacob's breathing and blood pressure.

"He seems to be doing well," the lead pulmonologist said. "The chest x-rays we took today, show that his lungs are healing well. Tomorrow we will try reducing the amount of oxygen and see how he does."

He saw uneasiness on her face. Before she could ask, he said, "We will watch him closely and make sure he is breathing properly. We just want to see if his repaired lung will do its job on its own again."

Amanda gave a slow nod of understanding and looked back at Jacob. *It has to happen, so why not start tomorrow, right?* She thought to herself.

After the doctors left, Amanda felt an urge to help her son but wasn't sure how. It wasn't like when he would scrape his knee, and she could kiss it better. No, it was much more severe, and yet the desire to help and soothe the pain was stronger too. Amanda determined that she would help keep Jacob clean. She asked the nurse if she could have a cloth. The nurse handed her one and asked what it was for.

"I just want to wipe his face and hair," Amanda said. "I want him to know I'm here, and he hasn't had a bath since his roll in the dirt. I thought I would try to help clean his hair out."

"We have some air dry shampoo if you would like," the nurse offered.

"That would be wonderful," Amanda said with a smile. *That would be rather handy in a travel bag,* she thought.

With a damp rag and a bottle of shampoo, Amanda set to cleaning her son.

Amanda thought people back home must be talking about Jacob because she got a lot of texts from family and friends throughout the day with wishes for speedy recovery and offering their support. It helped Amanda feel a little stronger.

Just before 4:00 pm, Amanda looked at Jacob's right hand and noticed that it looked swollen, and the fingernails were darker. Amanda brought it to the attention of the nurse. She came in and checked the IV and Jacob's wrist and hand. Then she notified the doctor. After a few minutes, the nurse disconnected the tubes from the IV in Jacob's right wrist and put the tubes in the IV in Jacob's left wrist.

Amanda waited nervously to see if that was going to make a difference. After 15 minutes the nurse came back to check on Jacob's hand, but it wasn't getting better. So the nurse removed the IV and raised Jacob's arm. By 4:45 pm, Jacob's arm was noticeably less swollen. Amanda was relieved, though she needed to walk a little bit to help her calm down.

Around 5:00 pm, Amanda went to the chapel on the second floor. She needed a break and a chance for some peace. Amanda sat quietly for five minutes. She tried to clear her head and just breathe. Then she prayed. She prayed for Jacob. She prayed for Jackson, for Ally and herself. She thought about the driver and what he must be going through. She prayed for him. Amanda knew from the texts and phone calls she was getting that others were praying for her too.

We are flooding the gates of heaven with our prayers, she thought to herself. That thought made her feel stronger somehow - to know that lots of people were praying and asking for the same thing. The common bond and unity she felt helped her realize she wasn't alone. She felt renewed and ready to go back and sit with her son.

Before she got to the PICU, she received a phone call from Whitney.

"Amanda, can you come down and visit for a minute?" Whitney asked. "We would like to give you something."

Amanda went down to the waiting room. She was happy to see Whitney and visit with her. Amanda told Whitney about her experience in the chapel and how she knew others were praying for her.

"There are a lot of people praying for you," Whitney said, a smile on her face. "I told people at my church about what happened, and we took up a collection today during the service. I have a check to give you. We know money will be tight, so we wanted to help."

She handed Amanda the check from her Baptist church. Amanda was shocked to see that it was for $500. She gave Whitney a hug, thanked her, and asked her to share with her congregation how much she and Jacob appreciated their help and prayers. When Whitney asked what else she could do, Amanda told her that Jacob would be going in for surgery on his pelvic bone the next morning. Prayers for a safe surgery would be welcome. Whitney said she would continue to pray for Jacob, and she would spread the word to all their girlfriends to pray with them. They visited for a while longer, and Whitney left.

Amanda prayed many times during the next few hours for everything to go well during the surgery. After another rough night of little sleep, Amanda was back by Jacob's bed just as they were taking him to surgery. The surgery was uneventful, and Jacob was resting comfortably by 9:00 am.

Around 1:00 pm, the team of pulmonologist came back

and explained that they would try reducing the ventilator to 85 percent and see what happened. Amanda watched attentively as they made the adjustment.

At first, it didn't appear to make much of an impact. For a minute, it seemed like Jacob would be fine with the reduced help from the machine. Then his breathing slowed, and his blood pressure fell. They quickly turned the ventilator up to 95 percent. Jacob's blood pressure and heartbeat normalized again after four tense minutes. Amanda couldn't look at the doctors. She just bent down and kissed Jacob's face, trying to control her own breathing again. Fear had gripped her heart when she saw the blood pressure fall.

The lead pulmonologist said, "That doesn't mean he isn't progressing, it just means his lungs still need more help. We will give him a day or so at this level of help and try again."

She didn't want to do that again. She knew they had to try to wean Jacob off the machines. She didn't want him to live his life in a drug-induced coma with machines doing everything for him. But how many times could she watch her son start to slip away? What if one of those times he doesn't come back?

It seems like I'm on this crazy ride, she thought to herself. *Just when it looks like things are improving, we start heading down again.*

She looked at Jacob and reflected on all that had happened in the past three days, especially the feelings she had received on Saturday morning.

"We will get through this," she said to Jacob, as she patted his hand. "I don't know how or what our life will look like in the future, but we will get through this."

Chapter 15

Comfort the Comfortless

Monday evening around 4:30 pm, a boy about 17 years old, was rolled into the PICU. They put him in the room next to Jacob's. Amanda could see heavy bandaging around his head. It wasn't too long before the parent's walked in crying. Their 14-year-old daughter was holding the mother's hand but walking slightly behind her. Amanda overheard some of the conversation. Something about the impact and possible brain damage. They would have to wait and see how he recovered once the swelling went down. Amanda heard the sobbing of the mother as the doctor walked away.

Amanda thought about how many families must come in and out of this unit. Far too many young lives were lost in this room, but many lives were saved by the skillful hands of the doctors and the grace of God.

That's the hard part in all of this, Amanda thought to herself as she leaned on Jacob's bed, her hand under his. *No one knows who the lucky ones will be until they survive. There is no rhyme or reason that we can see, but miracles happen for some and tragedy for others. Why? And why was she so fortunate to have an assurance that everything would be OK? Did others get the same feelings?*

Around 7:00 pm someone showed up to see Amanda. She went down to the waiting room and was surprised to see a woman from her church. Amanda recognized her but had to think quickly to remember her name. They had spoken only a handful of times. The woman was holding a large cloth bag in one hand and her purse in her other hand.

"Hi," Amanda said, "This is a pleasant surprise. What brings you all the way to Little Rock?"

"You," she said, matter-of-factly. "Ever since I heard about your son on Sunday, I haven't been able to stop thinking about you. I've said many prayers but wanted to do more. So I brought you some food."

"You didn't have to do that," Amanda said, shock and gratitude evident on her face.

"Well, I wanted to," she said with a wave of her hand. "You see, about 10 years ago, my husband had to be in the hospital for a week. It was really rough for a while, so I never left his side. I know a little of what you are going through. I remembered that you have a wheat allergy, and the hospital cafeteria is probably not prepared to give you many options. So I went to a specialty store here in Little Rock and picked up some things for you to eat."

"Wow," Amanda said in surprise. "To have you think of me is wonderful. Then to have you drive all the way up here and buy food, so I don't have to eat the same salad every day, is more than I could ask for. How can I repay you?"

"Don't worry about that," she said with a wave of her hand. "I remember getting the bill after my husband got home, too. You will have plenty of people to pay back. Just enjoy it, and that will be thanks enough."

Amanda took the food and put it in her locker. Then she went back to Jacob's room. As she was about to go into his room, Amanda made eye contact with the mother in the room next door. *I should talk to her,* Amanda thought to herself, but then dismissed the idea.

About an hour later, the woman got up to leave, and Amanda had the same thought. She couldn't ignore it anymore. She got up and followed her down to the elevators. Once inside, Amanda introduced herself and made small talk.

"Have you been to the cafeteria here yet?" asked the mother. "I need a break, and I'm hungry, but I'm worried I won't be able to eat anything here. I have Celiac's disease."

"Well, you will probably only be able to eat the salad,"

Amanda replied. "I have had it a few times because I have Celiac's myself. But someone just gave me some bagels and other good stuff we can try."

"I don't want to impose," the mother said.

"Not at all," Amanda said. "Someone gave it to me, and there is a lot of food there. Come on. You can try the salad next time."

The two woman ate a couple of bagels together and talked about where they were from and their families. Naturally, the conversation turned to why they were there in the hospital. Amanda shared a simplified version of Jacob's story. She tried to leave out the gore and graphic descriptions.

"He's in a drug-induced coma now and can't live on his own, but I hope to be able to speak to him again," Amanda said.

"I hope I get to speak to my son again," the mother said as she fidgeted with her purse. "He was riding on an ATV on a paved road. We don't know how yet, but somehow he fell off and hit his head really hard. He wasn't wearing a helmet."

The mother's chin wrinkled, and she quickly pulled out a tissue to dry her tears.

"He is in a coma, but not a drug-induced one," she began again. "The doctors don't see a lot of brain activity. We are worried we may lose him."

With these words, her crying began in earnest. Amanda put an arm around the woman's shoulders. Amanda wasn't sure what to say, but her heart wouldn't let her be silent.

"Can we pray together?" Amanda asked.

"Sure," the mother said. "I have been praying constantly."

"Dear Lord," Amanda began. "We are two grieving mothers with broken hearts and broken sons. Please help heal our sons, and our hearts. We trust in your grace and ask for peace to quiet our fears. In Jesus name, Amen."

"Thank you," the mother said. "I appreciate you sharing your food with me. I hope your son gets feeling better."

"I'm happy I didn't have to eat my dinner alone,"

Amanda said. "I'll pray for your son too."

On Tuesday, the doctor's came by to check on the boy that was in the ATV incident. The glass partition allowed Amanda a view of the machine they used to measure the brain activity of the unconscious boy. Amanda was familiar since she had seen the same machine used on Jacob to check his brain activity. The doctors had explained to her how it worked and what normal brain activity would look like.

Amanda didn't stare at the family or the doctors, but she did look at the monitor a few times as they were running the tests. She could see there was no brain activity. She looked at the mother and saw the heartbreak. The doctor said that if there isn't a change in activity by the next day, there would be no alternative but to turn off the machines that were keeping the young man alive. Amanda's heart broke for the mother and her family.

Amanda thought about the 2-year-old child that was rushed in only a couple days ago because a large entertainment center and TV fell on her. She had only seen and heard a few details as they wheeled the toddler past her room. She ached for that family too, but when she passed the mother in the lobby, Amanda said she was praying for her child. The mother said thank you and let Amanda know that the child was doing well and they hoped to be taking her home by the end of the week.

It was amazing and puzzling how so many kids could come and heal, while many others were not able to survive. It really made her appreciate the miracles when the kids did survive. She also marveled at the people that worked in this environment each day. They must have figured out how to block the emotions. Amanda hadn't been able to do that yet. She wanted to hug the mother of that young man next door.

Around noon, Jacob's temperature spiked to 102 degrees Fahrenheit. The nurse was coming in frequently after that to check how he was reacting to the Tylenol. After an hour it came down to 101.3, so the nurse gave Jacob a dose of Ibuprofen. By 3:00 pm, Jacob's temperature had returned to normal. It was about that time they replaced the Foley catheter that was removed earlier in the day. Amanda wondered if they were connected and what that would mean for Jacob later on. She hoped it wouldn't be long term. Amanda was glad to get some good news, though. They were able to reduce the amount of oxygen pushed by the machine to 50 percent. That meant that Jacob was breathing more on his own. They talked about possibly removing the breathing tubes in the next day or two.

Chapter 16
Life

Amanda passed the night in the family room again. On Wednesday morning she didn't go straight back to Jacob's bed. Amanda wanted to take a little time in the chapel. She had gone to the chapel a few times to pray and calm her mind. Today she wanted to give God a prayer of gratitude for helping Jacob get this far. The brain scans, the MRIs, and x-rays were all pointing to a good recovery.

The open door was inlaid with stained glass of no particular design, probably to keep the room as nondenominational as possible. In the front center stood pots with greenery. Above those on the front wall, which was painted an olive green, there were four framed stained-glass panes. They matched the design and pattern in the front door. Three circular lights hung from the pitched roof, with maroon beams against the white ceiling. At the front right, stood a podium. Amanda assumed it was for clergy to address families and friends that may be grieving. On the side walls were four white basket lights that let out light through the top and bottom. The 10 short, wooden benches were simply designed with a light stained finish.

Amanda had been in the room for 10 minutes and was getting ready to leave when the mother of the boy that had been in the ATV incident walked in. She was crying uncontrollably. Amanda knew intuitively what was wrong. She had experienced similar feelings when she watched her son leave with the life-flight nearly a week ago. He was so close to death, she felt sure he would be dead when she saw him next.

The mother sat down on a bench across the room from her. Amanda gave her a few minutes alone and offered a prayer for her while she waited. Amanda got up and walked over to her.

"I can tell you are struggling right now, can I help?" Amanda asked. She sat down next to her.

"Not unless you can bring people back from the dead," the mother sobbed but didn't look up. She recognized Amanda's voice.

"I'm sorry you lost your son," Amanda said softly. "Losing a child must be the worst pain a mother could ever bear."

There was silence for a little while, except for the sobs of the mother.

"I just don't understand why my son had to go now," the mother said with more passion and frustration than before. "I know your son is in a coma, but he's alive. My son hit his head on the concrete, and now he's gone! Why didn't he get saved when your son did? I prayed! I pleaded for God to take me instead! I asked for a miracle, and it never came. Why did he save your son and not mine."

Amanda didn't answer right away. She had asked herself the same thing and didn't really have a satisfactory answer. She knew she was blessed for getting her son back, though she wasn't sure what his life would hold now. To tell the truth, Amanda still worried that this mother's experience could still be her own. She couldn't think like that now. Amanda wanted to share the love she knew God had for this grieving mother. But how?"

"I don't know why God saved my son and not yours," Amanda said, still unsure of what her answer would be. "I can't answer for Him, but I know He loves both our sons the same. God has a plan for each of us, but sometimes that plan is shorter than we want it to be."

The mother turned to look at Amanda. It looked like she was considering what Amanda was saying.

"I don't know if it will help, but I know God understands what you are going through," Amanda said. "He watched his beloved son die for us. But like it says in the Gospel of John chapter three verse 16, if we believe in Christ, we won't perish in the end. We will have eternal life."

Both women sat in silence for a couple minutes. Each lost in her own thoughts. Then Amanda quietly got up and walked back down the hall to the PICU.

Amanda sat with Jacob and read to him for 15 minutes, then washed his hair again. Around 10:00 am, the pulmonologist came in and reduced the ventilator again. Amanda was excited to hear that the machine was only doing 35 percent of the breathing for Jacob now. That meant they would be able to remove the breathing tube altogether very soon. Amanda prayed again, thanking God for helping her son heal.

This feeling didn't last for long. Jacob's father walked in about that time. Amanda was gathering her stuff to leave when he stopped in front of her. His towering frame blocked her way out. Amanda was not interested in talking, so she asked him to let her through.

"I just want you to know this accident hasn't changed the custody arrangements," he said, not moving from his spot. "Nothing needs to change. When Jacob gets out of the hospital, I am still going to get my time with him."

"You can't take care of him," Amanda said, surprised he would suggest such a thing.

"I will hire a nurse to take care of him," he shot back. The conversation hadn't escaped the notice of the nurses, who were listening to the exchange.

"I am not going to discuss this now," she said and pushed her way past him.

The nurses reported the discussion to Esther, in Child Life Services. Before Jacob's dad left that day, she pulled him into her office and explained that while he is in the hospital around Jacob, he cannot argue with the mother.

"Research has shown that even patients in a coma can pick up on sounds going on around them," Esther said.

"You are risking a setback in Jacob's recovery by fighting in his presence."

"I wasn't fighting with her," Jacob's father said. He really didn't see the big deal. "I just wanted to let her know that I still have rights to see my kids."

"Our first priority here is to help our patients get well again," Esther said firmly, but not threateningly. "Any time a parent may hinder that process, through hysterics, shouting or interfering some other way, we must ask them to leave. If you feel you must argue about custody, make sure it's not around Jacob or Jackson. Jackson is hurting too."

"I understand," Jacob's dad said, and walked out of the office.

Chapter 17
Waking Up

On Wednesday morning, five days after the tractor incident, the pediatrician told Amanda that Jacob had reached all the milestones necessary for his recovery to bring him out of his coma. They were taking him off the ventilator that day, and the chest tube on the right side could be removed. They would also remove two of the four IVs that were in his arms.

"It's important that we allow his body to start to mend before we bring him out," the doctor explained. "Kids don't usually handle that much pain well. He is past the worst of the pain, so we can wake him up and help him recover more so he can go home."

"How long will it take for Jacob to come out of this coma?" Amanda asked, putting a hand on Jacob's arm. She was excited they were getting to have this conversation.

"Well, that depends," the doctor replied. "The body takes the drug and stores it in tissue and other places throughout the body. Even though we are slowly reducing the dosage, and even when we completely stop the medicine, his body has some of the drug stored up. It could be anywhere from four to 12 hours from the end of the dosage until he is awake and able to talk.

Amanda didn't like this wide range of possibilities.

"When will we know if he will come out of this coma?" Amanda asked, hoping he would clarify. "Will he wake up all at once or over time?"

"I'm optimistic that he will come out of it okay," the

doctor said, looking at the machines again. "He will be off the ventilator within the hour, and his brain activity seems good.

"As for how he will come out of the coma, we will see his motor skills come back first: finger movements, eyes opening and closing, and other reflexes," the doctor continued. "One of the last functions to come back is the cognition and speech. Interestingly, the hearing comes back really quickly, so we want to keep the room as quiet as possible. Soothing speech from you could be good. It will help him know you are here."

As promised, the right chest tube was removed. Then the nasogastric tube was removed. The arterial line IV in Jacob's right wrist was removed, and then the right-hand IV was removed.

Amanda let her ex-husband know that the anesthetist was going to have the medicine completely turned off around 2:00 am, though there would probably not be much to see until 7:00 or 8:00 am. She asked that he and Jackson be at the hospital around then, in case Jacob wanted to see Jackson. They decided Jackson would wait with Esther until Jacob was awake and talking.

On Thursday, Amanda was back up at Jacob's room at 5:00 am. She didn't want to miss a thing. It was at least a couple hours before the first signs of movement were seen. Amanda read to Jacob occasionally while she waited. Around 8:00 am, Jacob opened his eyes a little, though they didn't really appear to focus on anyone or anything.

Jacob's dad arrived a little after 8:15 am. They waited silently for another 30 minutes with little movement or change in vitals. Then at 8:42, Jacob opened his eyes and looked around a little. It was slow, but it was movement all the same. Amanda's smile nearly touched her ears for the joy she felt seeing her son moving on his own accord. She said his name and laid her hand on his. Jacob closed his eyes again and didn't open them again for five minutes.

This second time that he opened his eyes, it was a little faster and he started to look around a little more. His pupils were dilating and trying to focus on the people around him. His fingers twitched a little as Amanda lightly held his palm.

"Jacob?" Amanda said, choking back her tears. "It's Momma. Can you hear me? Can you see me?"

Jacob eventually nodded his head. Amanda realized she needed to ask fewer questions since he was probably still groggy and would not be able to answer all the questions she wanted to ask as fast as she wanted to ask them. She was thrilled though!

After about an hour, Jacob was moving a little more and seemed to register more of his surroundings. Amanda asked Jacob, "What do you want Jacob? Can we get something for you?"

It was silent for two minutes, as Jacob slowly turned his head to look at her and his dad.

"Brother," came the words, halting and raspy, from Jacob's mouth. "Where's Jackson?"

"He wants to see his brother," Amanda said. She knew their strong connection and understood Jacob's request perfectly. Amanda asked the nurse to call Child Life Services and ask Esther to bring up Jackson.

"She will bring him up, but she is talking to him briefly before they come to the PICU," the nurse said. "She has to prepare him a little for what he will see and hear."

Amanda understood and went back to Jacob's bedside.

"They are going to bring him up, just be patient," Amanda told Jacob as she again held his hand gently.

The drug was still having an effect on Jacob, so he closed his eyes and rested.

When Jackson came in, he made his way along the bed to stand next to Amanda at Jacob's side. Amanda wrapped her left arm around Jackson and left her right one on Jacob's hand. Jackson was grinning because Esther had told him his brother was awake and wanted to see him.

Jacob opened his eyes, more alert than before, and they smiled at each other. Amanda could tell that Jackson wanted to hug his brother, but that was almost impossible, so Jackson reached down and grabbed the hand Amanda was holding.

"I'm glad you are OK," Jacob said.

"I'm fine," Jackson said. There was a brief pause, and then Jackson leaned a little closer to his brother.

"I'm sorry," Jackson said, and his chin began to quiver. "I saw you drop your phone. And when you bent over to pick it up, Mr. Dave started moving again, and I didn't know why. I knew he had run over you, so I looked out the windows, trying to find you. When I saw you behind the tractor, I was banging on the window trying to make him stop. I'm sorry."

Amanda wrapped her arms around Jackson. Her heart was breaking for Jackson. It seemed like he felt guilty for what happened - as if he should or even could have stopped it sooner.

"I tried to bang on the window, but he was on the phone and wouldn't get off," Jackson continued, a few tears running down his face. "When he hit you with the blade, I started screaming, 'You just ran over my brother!' I'm sorry I didn't start yelling sooner."

Amanda looked into Jackson's face. While it was painful for Jackson, Amanda knew it was good for him to share his story with Jacob. She looked back at Jacob, and she could see that he was trying to make sense of everything.

"As Mr. Dave was stopping, I jumped out and ran straight to Dad," Jackson explained to Jacob. "When he came back, he picked you up, and you couldn't stand. I was praying for you while Dad was looking at you and your arm. We got in the truck and took off for the hospital. I'm sorry you got hurt."

"It's OK, brother," Jacob said with a slight smile. Then he turned to his dad and said, "I don't really remember what happened. There was a tractor and dirt, and then I woke up here."

That's a tender mercy, Amanda thought. *Will it always be that way, or will the memories suddenly come back one day? Who knew?* She would take it as a blessing for now.

"Momma?" Jacob asked.

"Yes, baby?" Amanda replied.

"Will I be able to climb up in my deer blind this fall and hunt?" Jacob asked, earnest in his question.

Out of reflex, Amanda laughed at the randomness of the comment but quickly followed it up with a sincere response. "Yes, you will be able to hunt, and go camping, and do the things you love. We will get you back to good as soon as possible."

"What's wrong with me," Jacob asked, clearly wondering why he was in the hospital.

Amanda could see that he was trying to piece things together. He could see that something had happened since he was last awake.

"Well, you were run over by a tractor," Amanda said, trying to think how much information would be good enough and yet not say too much to scare him. "The doctors have fixed your arm and some broken bones around your waist. Now we just need to help you heal and get you stronger, so you can do the things you love."

Jacob accepted that. He asked a couple more questions, but then complained about hurting. The doctor prescribed some pain medicine, and soon Jacob was falling asleep.

Amanda went down to the waiting room with Jackson when he and his dad were going to leave. She wanted to see how he was doing after seeing Jacob awake and talking. She could tell that his mood had lightened compared to the last six days. She was pleased to see that he wasn't worried after seeing his brother's condition and how raspy his voice sounded. After a short conversation, Amanda said goodbye to Jackson and went back to be with Jacob.

When Amanda was back in the room with Jacob, she pulled up the CaringBridge account to see if there was anything new on their message board. Amanda was amazed at how many strangers were offering prayers on their behalf. There were more than a hundred messages of prayers or well wishes. When Jacob woke up, Amanda read him a note from a US soldier that was stationed in Saudi Arabia.

"I learned about your accident from my family back in Northern Louisiana," Amanda read from the post. "I know that we are on different sides of the world right now, but I am praying you will be able to run again someday and that God will give you a speedy recovery."

"Wow, that's cool," Jacob said. "He doesn't even know me."

"Yeah, most of the people posting on here don't know you, but they are praying for you just the same," Amanda said. "That soldier has a lot to worry about, but he took some time to pray for you. That's awesome!"

Chapter 18

Bad Effect

Once Amanda went back up to the room, the rest of the morning and early afternoon went about the same as many others - Amanda reading to her son, doctors coming in to check on various systems and functions, and nurses taking vital signs and monitoring his condition. The biggest difference from the past week was now they could actually talk to Jacob. Once a doctor came in and asked Jacob what he thought was injured. Jacob responded, "Just about everything."

Around noon the doctors determined that it was time to stop the morphine drip and try another pain management drug.

Around 2:00 pm, Amanda's phone rang. It was her dad. He was calling to tell her they were almost at the hospital to see her. He brought her younger brother, Zachary, and Ally with him too. This was a pleasant surprise. She said she would meet them in the waiting room when they got there.

"Hello, baby girl!" Amanda exclaimed as she walked up to them in the lobby. "It's good to see you, Dad. I was hoping someone would bring up Ally, but I didn't want to make someone drive all the way up here."

"We're happy to do it," Eddy said. "I thought Ally would like a road trip."

"Momma, I drew you a picture," Ally said handing Amanda a piece of paper. Amanda looked at it and saw the colorful scribble marks across it. "Do you like it?"

"I love it, Sweetie!" Amanda said. She hugged Ally again,

grateful for this unexpected but much-needed visit.

"How is Jacob doing?" Eddy asked. "Any change?"

"Actually, yes, they brought him out of the coma today, and he talked to us for a little bit," Amanda said, grinning at the exciting news.

"That's great!" Eddy and Zachary said.

"Really, Mommy?" Ally said. "Can I see him now? I want to see Jacob."

"Oh, Sweetie, I don't think so - not yet," Amanda said, sorry to break her heart. "Jacob is doing much better, but I just don't think you are ready to see what he looks like right now. He has a lot of machines and stuff in his room, but in a few days, you might be able to see him."

"We've been having fun, haven't we Ally," Eddy said, wanting to change the subject so that Ally didn't get upset about not seeing Jacob. "Did you tell your mom what you got to do before we came up here?"

"We went to the store, and I picked out a present for Jacob," Ally blurted out, quickly forgetting the earlier disappointment. "It's a big green alligator!"

Amanda's eyes got wide, and she smiled to see the happiness on her daughter's face.

"That's great!" Amanda said as she tickled Ally, making her giggle. "Jacob's going to love that. It's not a live one, is it? They won't let me bring one up there."

"No," Ally said, giggling now at the silly thought of bringing a real alligator in the car. "It's a stuffed one. And it's really soft."

"That's great," Amanda said, "Jacob will love it."

Amanda's brother pulled the alligator out of a large bag sitting on the floor behind him. Amanda couldn't believe she had missed the large bag but figured she must have been too focused on Ally to have noticed it. The alligator was three feet long and dark green on top with a pale green underside.

"Do you mind if I deliver it to Jacob?" Zachary asked.

"Sure," Amanda said. "He's not really talkative, but he would love to see you."

Amanda led the way up to the PICU. Amanda

remembered going to a hospital to check on her little brother a little more than two years before. Zachary had been in a bad car accident that required jaws of life, a metal rod, and lots of stitches. Amanda was like his second mother. She was glad he was healthy again and hoped she would be able to say the same about Jacob in a year.

Zachary made up a tale about how he caught the huge reptile in the Mississippi and was sure Jacob could use the trophy in his hospital room. Amanda said she would have to hold onto it in her locker until they got a different room. They didn't allow toys and balloons in the PICU. The visit wasn't long, but Amanda was still thrilled that Jacob was awake and talking. She noticed that Jacob wasn't as talkative as she thought he would be, but assumed the new medicine might be making him tired, or maybe he was uncomfortable. They said, "Goodbye," and Amanda walked back down to the waiting area with Zachary.

Amanda enjoyed an hour with Ally and asked about how things were back home and how Grandma was doing. Eddy helped supply more information than Ally, but only after she took her turn. Eventually, Amanda said goodbye to Ally and went back to be with Jacob.

After she had got back to his room, Amanda saw Jacob's mood was worse. He complained about abdominal pain, and the nurse let the doctors know. They gave him a little more pain medicine. Finally, around 6:00 pm, she asked him if he was OK, but he didn't answer right away.

What is bothering him? Amanda wondered.

Then he said, "Why do they have my arms strapped down? Why can't I move?"

"I'm not sure, son," Amanda said, realizing that this might be what was bothering him. "Let me go ask the nurse."

Amanda walked over to the nurse and asked about the restraints.

"Well, he needs to be kept that way for a little while," the nurse explained. "When someone comes out of a coma after extensive surgery, he may try to get up and do things that might hurt himself. As we get more of the chest tubes and other instruments off of him, he won't be in as much danger and can move a little more. Does he fully understand the extent of his injury, especially to his pelvic bone and arm?"

"I told him his arm was sewn up, and his pelvic bone is broken, but I don't think he can understand everything that has happened to him," Amanda said and turned to look at Jacob. Jacob had a full scowl on his face now. Something was definitely wrong. "He seems to be more moody than usual. Jacob is usually more easy going than he is now."

"Maybe he is in pain," the nurse said, turning her attention to Jacob.

Amanda went back over to Jacob and put her hand on his arm. He tried to move away.

"What's the matter, baby?" Amanda asked.

"Don't call me baby," Jacob said. "I may be a prisoner here, but you can't call me a baby."

"You aren't a prisoner," Amanda said, trying to soothe him, but she could see he was trying to get away from her touch, so she took her hand away. "Are you in pain, Son?"

"Of course I am," Jacob said and raised his voice. "I want to get out of here."

"You can't struggle or try to move around, Jacob," Amanda said, sitting down on the rocking chair. She was trying to figure out what was going on. "You need to try and relax. You have been through a very difficult surgery, and you can hurt yourself if you aren't careful. Please just relax."

"Stop telling me what to do," Jacob yelled at her, and then said to the nurse. "Hey Jennifer, throw out the anchor and untie me."

"What?" Amanda asked in disbelief. The doctors had said the pain medicine could cause him to say strange things, like 'I want a cheeseburger at 2:00 am.' No one had told her he would be hallucinating.

"Mom, come here, I need to tell you something," Jacob said to her in a quiet whisper.

Amanda leaned over to get closer to his face.

"I love you," he said quietly. Then added, "Do you think she can hear me?"

"I don't think so," Amanda replied, completely confused.

"There is a ship coming," he said in a strange, husky voice with a crazy look in his eye. "We need to get off this boat."

Then the strange dialog started again. He yelled for the nurse to throw down the anchor, then quietly whisper to Amanda about a ship that was coming. Occasionally Jacob would add in comments such as, "I'm not in America! In two seconds my brain will explode!" and "I'll give you a million dollars if you see how fast you can chop my head off."

About the fifth time through the ship dialog, Amanda decided she had had enough. She couldn't take this any longer. As she left, the nurse closed Jacob's door so he wouldn't disturb the other patients. Amanda told the nurse to get the doctor to change the drug they were giving him. The nurse said she would, but before Amanda walked out, she demanded that the nurse write that on his chart. She never wanted to see her son act crazy like that again.

Amanda looked back at Jacob. The boy she just left wasn't her son. He seemed possessed. Amanda had never seen him act like this before. She could hardly recognize him with how crazy he was acting. Amanda couldn't stand seeing him like this, but she felt awful leaving him.

Amanda wasn't sure what had happened. She had watched her son lie on his back for a week unsure of whether or not he would come back to her. Now she couldn't recognize the boy in the bed. How many times can my heart break and my hopes get crushed before I lose faith altogether? she asked herself.

After walking in the hall for 30 minutes, she went back to the PICU. She stopped at the nurse's station. She could just barely hear Jacob in his room still carrying on about ships and getting off the boat.

"I'm sorry about what's happened," the nurse said. "Some patients have a negative reaction to that painkiller we were using at first, and it's obvious your son had a negative reaction. We changed the drug we are using to manage the pain, though it will take a while for the effect to wear off. Just as his body stored up the medicine that kept him in the coma, and it took time to work out of his body, this drug will take a while before it's fully out of his system."

"Why do you even have a drug that can cause hallucinations?" Amanda asked, accusation laced in the tone she used, her emotions raw from lack of sleep and the constant fluctuation in Jacob's condition.

"What works for some, will not work for others," she replied, keeping her tone even. "We have to keep options available so we can help each individual."

Amanda walked over to the glass room, with curtains drawn to hide the yelling child. Amanda was not ready to listen to him, even if the drug was wearing off. She didn't know how long it would take, so she stretched her legs some more. When she came back, he was asleep. The nurse suggested that Amanda get some rest too, so she went in search of a place to sleep.

Chapter 19
Moving In With the Sick

Around 11:00 pm on Friday night, Amanda went down towards the family room. She was hoping she would be able to find someplace to get some sleep. It had apparently been a busy day in the PICU because a lot of people were already camped out on the couches and floor. Amanda wasn't interested in sleeping in the middle of strangers if she could help it. She turned and went back down the hall, checking a couple doors. Finally, she found a room that wasn't locked. It was a conference room. It would probably be quieter than the waiting room anyway. She put her pillow down on the floor and laid down for a few hours of rest.

When Amanda got to Jacob's bed the next morning, the nurse informed her that they would be moving Jacob to another room that day. In preparation for transferring him, they would remove the Foley catheter and put Jacob in a diaper. Jacob was down to only two IVs and a chest tube. It was all progress.

As first, Amanda was excited that Jacob was doing well enough to be moved. When they moved him into a room that he had to share with another patient, Amanda was a little nervous. Jacob's dad, Jackson, and Amanda were there in the room as they got ready to move him.

In order to move Jacob to another room, the nurses showed Amanda how they would position the wheelchair next to Jacob's bed, raise the arm of the wheelchair and use a sliding board to create a bridge between the bed and wheelchair. One nurse carefully grabbed the sheet under

Jacob, while another nurse carefully grabbed Jacob to lift him up. They pulled him across the board and into the wheelchair. Amanda watched with concern and interest. In the back of her mind, she thought, *I hope I have a few people to help me move this big kid like they do.* But she dismissed the thought. She knew she would have to figure out how to move him on her own, but not today.

To make the move more difficult, Jacob had to hold a small pink tray that looked like a kidney bean. He threw up in it a couple times during the move and right after. The nurses said it was normal, potentially due to the injury and/or pain. It was only a concern if it was bloody or continued for a long time. Amanda hoped that would stop before they went home too. The nurses said it should subside in the next couple days.

They pushed Jacob down the hall and into the elevator. They went up to his new room on the fourth floor. While they were getting Jacob set up, Amanda heard the boy in the next bed coughing. Immediately, Amanda was not just nervous, but angry and anxious.

"What is the condition of the boy in the next bed?" Amanda tried to ask the nurse quietly so that Jacob or the other boy wouldn't hear.

"Sorry, I can't tell you that," said the nurse as she continued to set up Jacob's machines. "I'm not allowed to discuss the condition of other patients with people that are not their guardians."

"Can you tell me if you have put my son, who is not even a full 24 hours removed from a coma, in a room with a patient that is contagious?" Amanda asked more pointedly.

The nurse considered this for a moment and then finished setting up Jacob's machines and left.

Amanda was not through with the conversation though. She followed the nurse out into the hall and said, "Can you please answer my question? Should I be concerned that my son will die from pneumonia because you put him in a room with a contagious patient?"

"Ma'am, I can't discuss the condition of the other patient," the nurse responded, getting a little defensive. "I will check with the nurse in charge and see if we can or should change the room where your son continues his recovery. The room assignments aren't my decision, but I can look into it for you. I do know that we have a lot of patients right now, and getting a new room will probably not happen for weeks."

Amanda decided she needed to have some time with Jackson, so she left Jacob with his dad, and she went to the Camp Wannaplay area with Jackson. She enjoyed playing foosball with Jackson, but couldn't shake the nagging fear in her head. Will Jacob get sick? Will she still lose him because he is forced to be in a room with a boy that has a respiratory disease? Jackson asked her what was wrong, but Amanda didn't want him to worry. So she told him nothing was bothering her. They played for 30 minutes and then went back to the room. Jackson went with his father back to the hotel.

The next few hours were long and hard for Amanda. Every time the boy in the room coughed and hacked, she cringed and hoped that the air flow in the room didn't carry the germs to her son. She prayed that Jacob would be able to survive this ridiculous room assignment after all he had already been through. It just didn't seem right to fix him, just to put him in harm's way again.

Every time the nurse came in, Amanda would look at her in hopes that she would tell her that she was moving her son to another room. The nurse got quieter with each visit. At one point, Amanda pressed the nurse for an update on the chance they would be moved to another room. The nurse said the rooms were full, and there wasn't anything she could do to change the situation. Amanda tried to not let her worry show, but Jacob knew she was upset. He told her a couple times, "It will be okay, Momma. Don't worry about it. It will all work out."

Around 7:00 pm, the nurse came in to check on Jacob and get his vitals. She noticed that the chest tube site on Jacob's right side had some light saturation. The nurse noted it and then left. It was just before 9:00 pm when Amanda called the nurse back in. Jacob had just thrown up on himself and the bedding. The pads covering the right chest tube site were completely saturated now, so the nurse transferred Jacob to the wheelchair and took him into the bathroom. Amanda watched closely as she knew she would need to do this at home. The nurse cleaned Jacob and air dried the spots where he had incisions. She applied antibiotic ointments to Jacob's wounds and replaced the bandages. She removed the spoiled sheets and put new sheets on.

Once Jacob was back in his bed and recovered from the moving around, he felt much better. Amanda was not very comfortable though. This was a rough beginning to their time out of the PICU. She hoped it would get better. A new room without a contagious patient would be a great start.

That night, as Amanda started to fall asleep on the couch, she felt an alligator tale hit her in the face. Jacob had used his stuffed reptile to wake up Amanda. He smiled and said, "Mom, it's going to be OK. I have been praying, and I'm just sure that by noon tomorrow they will change our room."

"OK, Jacob," Amanda said, a smile coming across her face now. She was proud he had been praying for help. "They told us that there weren't any rooms, but you try to get some sleep now, OK?"

Around 4:00 am, Jacob woke Amanda up because he was uncomfortable. Amanda called the nurse in, and they tried to move him to help him get comfortable. It didn't help much, so the nurse started to give him some medicine to help with the pain. Just minutes after the dose was given, Jacob threw up. They changed his sheets again and cleaned him up.

"How are you feeling now," asked the nurse.

"Better, now that I've puked," Jacob replied, with a look of relief. After which, Jacob slept well for a few hours.

Around 8:00 am, the nurse came in to check on Jacob. Amanda hoped she would tell them Jacob would be moved to another room, but she didn't say anything. Instead, the nurse walked Amanda through how to properly change bandages, what to look for, and how to clean them. While still annoyed by the coughing in the background, Amanda was hoping this instruction meant they would be going home within a week or so. That was something to look forward to, though the task of caring for Jacob alone in this state was daunting. Amanda tried to pay attention to the cautions and instructions.

As the morning wore on, Amanda was hyper sensitive to Jacob's breathing. She worried that any minute he would develop a cough. What would violent coughing do to his recovery and stitched up wounds? She even started to wonder if she was getting sick. She pushed that thought away though, knowing she couldn't get sick now. Amanda also wondered what would happen to Jacob's faith if they weren't moved. She again prayed for their prayers to be answered and get them to a room that was safer for his recovery.

At 12:01 pm, right before lunch was brought around, the nurse came in and started to unhook some of the machines connected to Jacob.

"We have a new room for you, Jacob," the nurse told him. "You will have your own room."

"I'm happy for the change, but why are you changing now and not yesterday?" Amanda asked as the nurse continued to get things ready.

"As far as I know, we just needed to make sure the paperwork was in order for a private room," she replied. "I'm sorry you had to wait so long to get an answer."

"Well, I just hope Jacob doesn't get sick," Amanda said, grabbing her things. She could tell that the nurse was either in a bad mood or was upset by something. Amanda didn't want to come off ungrateful, so she added, "I'm happy that we got the paperwork straightened out so the move could be made now. Thank you."

Chapter 20

Starting the Transition Home

The nurse moved Jacob into the wheelchair, much like they had done the day before. Jacob still felt nauseous, but only threw up once this time. When Jacob was settled into his new room, the nurse gave him some medicine to help with the nausea. As Jacob rested, Amanda offered a prayer of gratitude for getting their room changed. She remembered Jacob's comment the night before. This experience was changing him too.

Jacob took a nap for an hour. Around 3:00 pm, the nurse came in and started talking about getting Amanda and Jacob ready for going home. This made Amanda really excited, but she also felt anxious. The nurse didn't know exactly when Jacob would be discharged, but part of that depended on getting Amanda comfortable with taking care of Jacob's needs.

Amanda knew she could and would do it. She had taken care of her brother when she was 15-years-old when their parents were gone on jobs or elsewhere. She knew she would do anything to take care of her son, but she just wanted to make sure Jacob was comfortable.

"First, I know you have been here when we had to change his diapers," the nurse began. She wasn't going to beat around the bush. Jacob's face went red. "As his body gets healthy, he will gain control of his bladder and intestines, but the trauma, surgery and pain killers are making all that really difficult for him to control. As you watched, you probably noticed it's not like changing a baby's diaper. He is much bigger than a baby, and we can't lift him up like a baby. You have to roll him to clean and wipe him up. Then pull out the old diaper, and put in a new one."

The nurse had Amanda try. She had been watching, so she did pretty well.

"Something you have to remember while he is recovering, he may spend a lot of time in bed," the nurse said. Amanda saw Jacob shake his head. She knew he wanted to get out of bed. "We have been moving him and repositioning him each time we come in to check vitals. It's important to move him every 30 to 45 minutes during the day. If you don't, he will get bed sores. Once he spends less time in bed, it won't be as critical."

Jacob was ready to get up and run now. He didn't want to be in a bed for 12 hours or more. Amanda knew he had gone an hour or two during the night without disturbances, so she assumed this 30 to 45 minutes must be if Jacob was in bed all day long. She wouldn't get lazy on Jacob though. She would get up during the night if she needed to. She hoped she had the strength to do it.

"Now, we need to get Jacob into the wheelchair and take him out to get some fresh air," the nurse said, as she went to the corner to retrieve his wheelchair. "As I'm sure you guessed, we can't go home with you, so you will have to learn to do this on your own. I will be here to help guide you, but I want you to do as much as you can."

This exercise - for it was a major exercise since Jacob was only a few inches shorter than her and weighed as much as her - was more difficult. The nurse would coach her and make sure Amanda didn't do anything without being secure and safe. They started by putting the chair next to Jacob's bed, locking the wheels and lifting the arm closest to Jacob's bed. Then the nurse helped Amanda position the sliding board between the bed and wheelchair. The nurse pointed out that the sheet under Jacob should be used to help him slide on the board. Amanda struggled to coordinate grabbing the sheet, holding Jacob, and moving him down the board. It took about 30 minutes to move Jacob to the wheelchair. When Amanda was done, she needed to sit down and rest. The nurse quickly checked all the tubes and lines to make sure nothing was obstructed.

"This sheet is your best friend," the nurse said, lifting the blue sheet that was under Jacob. "You should use it to let Jacob slide on the board. Don't try to be she-woman and dead lift him all the time. You won't be any use to your son if you are in the hospital with a hernia."

Amanda didn't answer. She was struggling to understand how she was going to manage on her own. She had a three-hour drive with potential stops. She couldn't try to take him to the bathroom at a gas station in this condition. She had to set up his bed and get the house ready for Jacob. She needed to find a way to get him into the house which wasn't wheelchair ready. Taking Jacob out of a car would not be as easy as getting him out of a bed that could be moved up and down. She tried to get her bearings and resolved to put one foot in front of the other. She decided to start making a list of things that needed to happen, and then either work on them or ask others to help out with the tasks.

Amanda pushed Jacob down the hall and into the elevator so she could take him to the Camp Wannaplay area. When they got there, they saw that there was a four-legged animal in the area. As they got closer, Amanda saw a little sign above the waist-high swinging door that said, "This is Oscar. He's part of the TAILS program." Then in smaller print towards the bottom it read, "TAILS = Therapeutic Animal Intervention Lifts Spirits."

Amanda thought this would be great. Jacob loved dogs and animals. There were only two other kids in the area, and one was not interested in the dog. Once the other little boy finished petting the dog, Amanda pushed Jacob closer to the docile golden retriever. Jacob petted the dog and asked the caretaker questions about how old he was and where he stayed most of the time. Amanda sat on a bench that was under the window and watched Jacob enjoy the dog. When Jacob looked at Amanda, his expression changed. He seemed to get sad again. Amanda pushed him to the outdoor portion of Camp Wannaplay. The sunshine felt good on their faces. It was the first time Jacob had been outside in a week. This helped a little, but Jacob still looked a little sad.

"What's wrong Jacob?" Amanda asked, sitting on a bench next to Jacob. "Didn't you like petting the dog?"

"Yeah," Jacob said.

Amanda knew she shouldn't pry too much or make him talk before he was ready. It seemed like this mood was just starting today.

"Are you hurting or are you upset about something that happened today?" Amanda asked, telling herself she would leave it alone if he didn't want to talk about it.

"I saw how hard it was for you to move me," Jacob said, his gaze never leaving the ground. "I'm sorry it's hard on you."

"Oh, sweetie, it's going to be fine," Amanda said with a little laugh. She was glad he told her, but she knew she needed to help him not feel bad about what happened. "I will get better at moving you the more times I do it. I'm going to be strong when you get to walking again."

Amanda flexed her arms and put on a tough face as she said this last sentence. Jacob looked at her and laughed too. They sat there for just five minutes or so, and then Jacob asked to go back to his room.

Once back in the room, the nurse helped Amanda get Jacob back in bed, and Jacob slept for an hour. Amanda decided she would use this time to start a list of things that needed to be done before they returned home.

Mentally she went through the process of taking Jacob home. She tried to think about what would be different and what changes she could make to make life easier for them or more like the hospital. She had a one story house so they wouldn't need an elevator, but there were small steps and thresholds, making it difficult for a wheelchair. She wrote down, 'Make a ramp.'

She thought about food and assumed that when they sent him home, he would be able to go back to normal foods. She would have to ask about that. She made a note.

She looked at Jacob and all the times she had tried to clean him up. It was the best she could do, but she would have to give him a bath. The nurses hadn't talked about showers or baths yet, but she was pretty sure they wouldn't want her to put him on the ground. She would probably need to get a chair, and spray him down. That led her to think about how their shower head wasn't sufficient for washing off someone that couldn't move around under the water. She needed a shower head that moved around the person. She wrote down, "Install hand held shower head."

Amanda continued to think and jot down notes, trying to be thorough so she wouldn't have any surprises.

Chapter 21
Up and Down

After Jacob had got his dinner, a nurse came in to explain how to continue Amanda's education about taking care of Jacob at home. She brought in a strange looking chair and a clear, plastic jug.

"I know you will want to take a shower after you get home," the nurse said to Jacob. Jacob nodded his head. Then the nurse turned her attention to Amanda. "That's good. Keeping him clean is important, but we want to make sure he is safe in the process."

The nurse walked Amanda over to the bathroom in the room.

"I'm sure you have noticed the shower chair in here," the nurse began again. "You will use a similar chair in your house to give him baths. You will follow the same procedure you used moving Jacob to the shower chair as you would any other chair. While he has open wounds, you should never give him a bath. Do not submerge the incision. Once you are finished giving Jacob a shower, you need to be careful not to rub the incisions or stitches. You should use your hair dryer to dry those areas thoroughly."

Amanda listened intently. The hair dryer idea made sense to her. She wondered how it would all work in her house with a much smaller bathroom, but she would figure it out. The nurse walked out of the bathroom with Amanda and picked up the clear jug.

"This bottle is for when Jacob feels the urge to urinate, but can't make it to the bathroom in time," the nurse said. "The diaper will work too, but you will find cleaning a jug is easier than changing a diaper for a 10-year-old boy."

"Yeah," was all Amanda could say, trying to figure out how Jacob would use that without making a scene. Jacob's eyes widened. The thought of diapers wasn't quite as bad as before.

"You can just keep this jug with you in your wheelchair at home," the nurse said, either not noticing or used to the looks on their faces. "For boys, it's pretty simple; just point and shoot. As you continue to heal and get back to life, your bladder control will improve, and you won't need it as much."

The nurse put the chair closer to Jacob and Amanda. Amanda saw that it was all white, had a plastic bench with an egg shaped hole. There was a bar across the back with a pad on it, and two arm rests. The frame appeared to be aluminum.

"One of these will be delivered to your house before you go home," the nurse explained. "You won't actually be using a regular toilet for a while, Jacob. You will need to use this chair if you can make it. It is just too hard to get you on and off a normal toilet, so until you can walk around and control your bowels a little more, you will need to use this chair."

Then the nurse explained that the arm could be moved down to make the transition easier from a wheelchair.

Amanda looked at Jacob. She could tell that he was not looking forward to using the chair. He wasn't fond of wearing diapers and getting cleaned up, but he looked at the chair with a look of disgust and dejection. Amanda was glad they would have something like that. It would be easier to use than a normal toilet. There would be a lot of adjustments to make when they got home.

The nurse asked if they had any questions. Amanda said she didn't and Jacob didn't answer. As she prepared to leave, she reminded them they could ask her questions later if they thought of any. After the nurse left, Jacob sat back and closed his eyes.

"I know you aren't looking forward to using that toilet chair," Amanda said, searching for a way to help her son cope. "But look at it this way, it won't last forever. Only you and I will be in the room to see how it is used. We will make sure there aren't any signs or smells that tell others what it's for.

Jacob looked at her but didn't show any sign at feeling better about it.

"Maybe we can find a way to cover it, or draw on it so it will look cooler," Amanda said, hoping Jacob would look at it a little different.

"I'll get used to it, I guess," Jacob finally said. "I don't know how cool you can make a toilet chair. I just hope I can get to walking soon, so I don't have to use that seat for a long time."

Around 7:00 pm, Amanda decided she needed to go for a walk. She wasn't sure why, but the thought of going home had reminded her that she would have to deal with custody rights. She remembered the conversation Jacob's dad had started in the PICU a week ago, saying this wasn't going to change anything, and he would pay for someone to take care of Jacob at his home. But Amanda wasn't about to keep the same arrangement they had before the tractor incident or give Jacob to his dad for care by a stranger. She wasn't sure what she could do, but she wanted to know her options. She went down to the third floor Atrium Garden to make a phone call.

Amanda called her lawyer and told him what had happened in the PICU.

"I know he is going to try and take Jacob back at his first opportunity," Amanda said, her anxiety over the situation growing as she spoke. "I don't think that will be good for him, and it's not going to be good for me. The Child Life Services specialists are worried he is downplaying the situation. I need to keep Jacob until he is better, and then I never want to go back to losing my kids for two weeks again."

Her attorney explained that after a traumatic experience

like this, she could make a motion to have custody changed, and the judge would probably grant it without a formal hearing. The sooner she acted the easier it would be to get those changes made.

Amanda asked him to make the motion so she could have her kids during the week and every other weekend. She hoped the motion passed as easily as her lawyer said it could. Not only would she get her kids more often, but she wouldn't have to spend a lot of money to make it happen. She knew she was already swimming in debt. In the back of her mind she knew it wasn't going to be easy, but it would be worth it.

That night was the best Amanda had spent in the hospital. She could sleep on a couch next to Jacob's bed. There wasn't another child coughing in the room. She was used to the machine noises, and the nurses didn't come in as often as they did during the day. Maybe she would feel more stable after a decent night's sleep.

Chapter 22
Sore Foot

Amanda woke up on Monday morning with the sun shining. She felt better than she had in almost a week. Jacob had slept well that night, too. Amanda heard from some family and friends that they would be coming up to visit. Amanda thought this would be a great day.

During breakfast, Amanda noticed that Jacob was moving his left foot more than usual. She asked him about it, but he just shrugged and said it was just uncomfortable. Around 9:00 am, Jacob started to complain that his foot hurt more. Amanda got up and pulled the sheet back. She found the sheets soaked with blood tinged fluid.

Amanda called the nurse, and she came in to inspect his left foot. The IV site they had been using was oozing fluid. The skin around it was red and slightly swollen. The nurse let the doctor know and was given orders to take out the IV and not restart it. Taking out the IV was more painful than having it in. The nurse had a little difficulty removing the IV, but she got it out and bandaged Jacob's left foot. The pain in Jacob's foot abated a little, but it was still sore.

Around 10:00 am, Granny arrived with a couple of Amanda's aunts and cousins. They visited with Jacob for a little while. It was a pleasant diversion for Jacob and Amanda. While they were there, the nurse let Amanda know that Jacob needed to be taken for chest and spinal x-rays. Amanda used this as a chance to practice transferring Jacob to a wheelchair. It was smoother than the last time, but still not easy. The women talked about things

going on back home while Jacob was gone.
The nurse brought Jacob back in 20 minutes after taking
him. The doctor said that the x-rays showed that Jacob's
lungs and back were healing well. It was music to Amanda's
ears.
Because Jacob's lungs looked like they were healed, the
second chest tube was removed. The site had been leaking a
little anyway, so the nurse cleaned the area and applied fresh
bandages. The nurse checked all of Jacob's other bandages.
In order to check all the sites, the nurse, Amanda, and
Granny all helped to roll Jacob from one side to the other so
the dressings could be changed. The nurse found that the
site of his right chest tube had soaked through the gauze and
gotten his gown wet. The cut under Jacob's left arm looked
good though and appeared to be healing properly. The site
of the pelvic bone surgery was healing well too.
After Granny and other family members had left, a
woman came in to visit with Amanda. She introduced
herself as a hospital teacher. She helped patients keep up
with their education while in the school or transition back
to their school program back home. They discussed Jacob's
situation and that they hoped he would not have a long-term
recovery. Amanda wanted Jacob to be able to go back to
school as soon as practical so he wouldn't get too far behind.
The hospital nurse said there was a home-bound program
in Louisiana that would allow him to have a teacher come
to him until he was able to go back to school again. Jacob
was already enrolled in his fifth-grade class back home. The
hospital teacher would leave a referral form with the doctor,
and Amanda would have to follow up with the school. The
hospital teacher would try to contact the school as well since
it would be easier to get paperwork filled out and sent back
with Amanda at discharge.
After the hospital teacher had left, Amanda made a phone
call to the superintendent for their school district. He helped
her find out who she needed to talk to. When she finally got
the lady over the program on the phone, Amanda learned
that this program wouldn't apply to her son's situation.

That didn't make sense with what Amanda had just learned. Amanda thought she should contact her cousin who was working on her master's degree in education down in Baton Rouge. Amanda sent her an email explaining what the hospital teacher said, what her school board member said, and then asked her cousin if she knew anything else about the program. Amanda also asked her cousin what else she could do to help Jacob get into this program. Once the email was sent, Amanda would just have to move on to something else and wait to hear back later.

Amanda took some time while Jacob was resting to search online about the Louisiana homebound program and how it worked. The information she found was a little vague, but she learned about some things she needed to ask her cousin and the school board member later when she was home.

Jacob and Amanda went for another walk around the hospital after dinner. Amanda took him to the atrium garden this time. After looking around for a little while, Amanda decided to take Jacob back towards the PICU. She wanted to show him the cool murals painted on the walls leading up to the PICU. There were scenes of kids playing on swings, fishing in ponds, building snowmen, and climbing in trees. Some of the kids were three dimensional and came off of the wall a few inches. They admired the great detail in the scenes.

A nurse walked up as they were looking at the walls.

"The really cool thing is each child depicted in the murals is a former patient of the PICU," the nurse said, stopping to admire the wall with Amanda and Jacob.

"That's really cool," Jacob said. "How long has it been here?"

"Let's see," the nurse said, looking up as he thought. "I think it was completed in 2004."

Amanda and Jacob thanked him as he went into the PICU. After a couple more minutes admiring the murals, they went back to Jacob's room so he could rest again.

Chapter 23
Birthday in the Hospital

On Tuesday morning, the nurse came in to do a routine check on Jacob. Amanda looked at her phone and realized it was her birthday. *I'm a big girl now,* she thought to herself. *I don't need a celebration for my birthday. My son is alive, and that's the greatest gift of all.*

Jacob asked the nurse what day it was. When the nurse answered, he said, "Hey, that's your birthday, right Mom? Happy Birthday! I bet you haven't had a birthday in the hospital before. Sorry, we aren't at home or somewhere better."

Amanda was surprised that Jacob remembered it was her birthday.

"You're getting better, and that's all that matters," Amanda said. "Maybe your uncle will bring me a cool pink alligator to match yours."

She did get another gift, though it wasn't a pink alligator. At 2:00 pm, the nurse came in to remove Jacob's feeding tube. It was the last of the tubes.

Amanda decided Jacob needed a change of scenery and let the nurse know she wanted to take Jacob to Camp Wannaplay or the atrium garden. Jacob said he wanted to see if there was a dog in the Camp Wannaplay area. They went down, and Jacob was in luck. He got to see another dog from the TAILS program. It was a good break for both Amanda and Jacob.

At 3:00 pm, a nurse came in to tell Amanda that someone was there to see her in the conference room by the waiting room. Amanda thought it might be Granny and Ally, but they usually called her and let her know they were coming. When she got down to the door she was told to go in, Amanda smiled to herself because it was the room she slept in the previous Saturday night.

When Amanda walked in the room, she saw Ally, Jackson, all her girlfriends, Granny, Eddy, Zachery and brother and sister Ratley. Amanda was so surprised. She wasn't expecting people to even call her that day, let alone make the drive up to see her on her birthday. She laughed and asked what everyone was doing there, though she knew the answer from the decorations. There were colorful helium balloons held down by strings, party hats, streamers, cards, gifts wrapped and sitting on the table, and a cake with her name on it. Everyone broke out into a spirited, if not in-tune, rendition of the "Happy Birthday" song. Amanda gave hugs to her friends and kids while the song was sung. She felt really loved by the sacrifice these people made to come and visit her on her birthday.

She opened the cards, each contained a sweet message. A few cards had cash in them. One of the gifts was a deck of cards.

"I didn't want you to forget Pokeno night, though we understand if you can't be there for a couple of months, Amber said, explaining the reasoning behind her gift. "You and Jacob can play in the room, too, if you want."

Another gift was a miniature Angel One helicopter. That was a gift from Granny, to help Amanda and Jacob remember the miracle better.

Amanda felt overjoyed with the support. When someone mentioned that the cake was gluten free, Amanda smiled, while a few faces looked a little disappointed. They all had a piece and visited with Amanda. Amanda took a group of friends and family back to see Jacob in his room. Ally and Jackson were part of the group that went to see Jacob. Jackson was happy to see that his brother was doing better.

Ally had not seen Jacob in almost a month. Jacob was free of most of his IV's and all the tubes, so when Ally asked to get closer, Amanda could set Ally on the bed next to Jacob. She cautioned her to be careful since Jacob was still hurt. Ally held Jacob's hand, and they smiled at each other. Jacob asked Ally about Mom's birthday surprise, and Ally happily told him all she could. Just before most of the group left, Ally laid down next to Jacob. She didn't say much, but Amanda could tell that Ally missed her big brother. Amanda couldn't wait to have everyone home again.

Jacob was happy to hear that his mom got a birthday party. Eddy and Zachery stayed with Jacob to keep him company. They thought that would help Amanda feel better about going to dinner with everyone else.

Amanda was excited to go out to eat, but it was difficult to leave her son. He had made so much progress she thought she could leave, but she hadn't left the hospital in 11 days. Going out with friends and family made Amanda feel like life was almost normal again. The stress wasn't consuming her. She was able to relax and have a good time. She focused on Ally and Jackson, which felt good.

After an hour and a half, they all started walking back. In the lobby, Granny gave Amanda a gift. It was a hotel room key; the room was already paid.

"It will allow you to have a good night's rest, take a shower, and just relax a little," Granny said. "You look so worn out. You need to take care of yourself too, you know."

"I don't have time for that," Amanda said in a joking tone. "Thank you, Granny!"

"It's room 204," Granny said while pointing at the plastic room keys. "But you can see it written on the key envelope. Oh, yeah, and here are your car keys. Since you said you would be leaving the hospital in the next day or two, we brought your car up for you."

Amanda said thank you and took her keys.

They all said goodbye, and Amanda went back up to see Jacob.

At 9:00 pm, Amanda told Jacob about the hotel room she was given. She said she would go take a shower at least and possibly even get a good night's rest. Amanda wasn't sure if she would be able to make herself stay, no matter what the good reasons were, but she didn't want to make up her mind yet. Maybe she would feel more comfortable about it all after a decent shower.

By 10:15 pm, Amanda was back in the hospital room with Jacob. She did get a good shower, and it felt good to not feel rushed like she was monopolizing the bathroom in the family room at the hospital. When she considered staying in the room, she knew she wouldn't be able to sleep. Jacob was doing a lot better than he had been, but she didn't want to be away too long. If anything happened, she was at least 15 minutes from getting to his room, and he wasn't being watched over as closely as he was in the PICU. The biggest reason she couldn't stay in the hotel was that she didn't want Jacob to feel alone. She wanted him to know she was there for him always.

"Why didn't you sleep at the hotel, Momma?" Jacob asked when she came back in.

"I wanted to be here with you," Amanda replied, as she sat on the stiff green and white couch she would be sleeping on. She added with a smile, "And this couch is so much more comfortable than any bed."

Jacob smiled and said, "Should we talk to the doctors to see if they will send it home with us?"

"Maybe," Amanda said, ruffling his hair. "I think we will have plenty of furniture to add to our house from our stay here. We should probably let the hospital keep the couch."

"Happy Birthday, Momma!" Jacob said.

"Thank you," Amanda replied. "It was a good day. I think I'd rather go camping next year."

They both agreed that would be better than celebrating in the hospital.

Chapter 24

Going Home

The discharge from the hospital for Jacob came right after lunch on July 28, 2010. Both Amanda and Jacob had a pent up excitement that morning as they waited for details about when Jacob could go home. Jacob was anxious to go home, though he was starting to realize that even home wouldn't be as carefree as he remembered it. It wasn't just the hospital that was dull and boring for his young mind, it was the fact he had to sit or lay all the time. That would have to continue at home. Still, it was a change of scenery.

Amanda, on the other hand, was thinking through her list of things that needed to be done. The hospital bed, bath chair, and hand-held shower head would be installed that day by her dad, brother, and other family members. Amanda also said she would go by and double check the equipment when it arrived. She would follow up with the school board, but they had a week to work on that before school started. She had asked her dad and brother to build a little ramp to the side door under the carport. They said they would have it done, and she would get to see it when she got home. She would have to come back up to Little Rock the following week for a follow-up appointment with the oncologist. She could start physical therapy with Jacob the week after that. Amanda remembered that she had to deal with the bunk beds and boxes of stuff she left piled up in the middle of the room on the mattresses nearly two weeks ago when she was painting the boys' room. She wouldn't get around to decorating for a long time, but that was okay. As

long as they had somewhere to sleep, they would make it
through.

What she hadn't figured out, was how she would survive.
The bills were sure to come, and after all the attention they
had received, she was sure it would take two lifetimes of
full-time work to pay off this hospital stay. The Medicaid
insurance she was on would cover some of this stuff, but
there was no way it would cover everything. She didn't
even know if she would have a job. The job situation was
complicated. After some reflection during the more quiet,
restless hours in the hospital at night, Amanda wasn't sure
if she was really in the right profession. Her degree and
experience were in office management. She had run the
books for her ex-husband's farm when they were married
and did it well. It wasn't just the job, though, she was getting
a nagging feeling in her mind that she should move on. The
weight of massive debt she was about to receive had made
her push that thought away. She would have to deal with
that later when Jacob didn't need her all the time. Taking
care of him was the only job she could focus on right now.

"Are you excited to go home?" Amanda asked Jacob,
hoping the conversation would help her mind calm down.

"Yes, I want to go home," Jacob replied with a smile. He
poked around at the food on his lunch plate. "How long do I
have to stay in a wheelchair?"

"The doctor said non-weight bearing for 4-6 weeks,"
Amanda said, pulling out her phone to look at her calendar.
"That means at least three more weeks. That's as early as
you can start standing to try and learn to walk again. It
won't come back immediately."

"So that means I can start trying to walk towards the end
of August, beginning of September?" Jacob asked, trying to
figure it out in his head.

"If everything goes well, we should be able to start
physical therapy after the 20th of August," Amanda said,
counting the weeks from the pelvic surgery and then adding
a little time for setting up doctor's appointments. "When you
go for therapy on your legs and waist, they may also start

rehab with your arm, but we'll see how it goes."

"Do you think I will be walking before my birthday?" Jacob asked, an excited look in his eyes.

Amanda had to think for a minute. She had been told repeatedly by Esther and other Child Life Services specialists not to lie. As a mother she wanted her child to be optimistic and get better as quickly as possible. The doctors hadn't spoken of walking happening quickly. They had said that if the bone healed, he should be able to walk again. While no other bones were broken, Jacob would have to learn to build up coordination, muscle mass, and endurance over a long time. It all depended on how Jacob healed and worked at it.

Amanda looked into Jacob's eyes. The smile was starting to fade because she took too long to answer.

"Well, we don't know for sure how long it will take you to walk again," Amanda began. When Jacob started to look away, she quickly went on. "But if you want to be walking by the end of September, I will be right here with you to make that happen."

Jacob smiled up at his mom, and she smiled back.

At 12:45 the nurse came in with a bag and some paperwork. She handed the bag to Amanda and started to go over the discharge paperwork. Amanda was really excited but listened carefully for any information that would help her keep Jacob comfortable. The nurse said Jacob would only have a small amount of prescription pain medicine to take home. This was so he wouldn't become addicted which Amanda appreciated. She wasn't sure how well the over-the-counter pain medicine would keep up with Jacob's pain, but they would have to deal with that. The nurse pointed to a document Amanda had in her bag that discussed ways to help children cope with pain.

The nurse went over the proper cleaning guidelines for bathing and wound care. This was a review and went quickly. Then she covered some nutrition points and things to watch for regarding mood swings and adjusting to life with a wheelchair. All that seemed easy to follow - nothing earth shattering. After a brief pause for questions, the nurse continued to move on with the paperwork that needed to be signed so Jacob could go home.

At 1:00 pm, Jacob was wheeled downstairs. Jacob saw the two fish tanks in the front entry way and asked to look at them for a minute. Amanda noticed the pure joy on Jacob's face as he watched the bass and catfish swimming around. A little bit later she wheeled him out to the curb where Amanda was able to load him into her car. She now realized that the transporter at the hospital was taking the wheelchair back inside. She hadn't realized she would be without a wheelchair for the entire three-hour trip down to her house, where their wheelchair was. Well, that would mean she couldn't make any bathroom breaks.

What if Jacob needed to go to the bathroom? she asked herself. Then the jug came back to her mind.

It will be a sink or swim experience with the jug, Amanda thought. She immediately regretted the water reference as she hoped it would be a dry drive home.

"Well, Jacob," Amanda said once she got in the car. She found the jug and handed it back to him. "We don't have a wheelchair, so you will have to use this if you need to go during the drive. You just went before we left the room, and I will go straight home, but if you feel the need, that jug is your only option. I won't be able to change your diaper until we get home, so soaking yourself would not be ideal. Sorry."

Jacob blushed a little and looked out the window. After only 20 minutes into the drive, Amanda looked back, and Jacob was asleep. He stayed that way most of the drive home. Half an hour away from home, Jacob had to figure out the jug. He made it work but was glad it was not far away. He was really embarrassed when he needed to use it, but Amanda was happy he figured it out. They would just dump it when they got home.

Amanda had called ahead to Granny and Eddy to let them know they were leaving the hospital, by the time Amanda had arrived at her house, there were a few family and friends there to welcome her and Jacob home. Ally was with her grandma and was one of the first to run up to Amanda when she stepped out of the car. Jackson was with his dad but would be coming later that evening.

Zachery brought out the wheelchair for Jacob. Amanda opened Jacob's door and positioned the wheelchair by Jacob's seat. After lifting the arm on the wheelchair, she positioned the slide board between the seat of the car and the wheelchair. Then she slid him out of the car and onto the wheelchair. The family watched, willing to help, but unsure of where to lift and how to assist. They just looked on and welcomed Jacob home. Jacob used his right arm to help when possible, though Amanda did most of the lifting.

Zachery offered to push Jacob into the house and started towards the side door with the ramp while Amanda grabbed her purse from the car, and they went inside. Others helped grab bags and stuffed animals. As they walked in, Amanda inspected the ramp. She was impressed with the ramp her dad and brother built. She was glad she wouldn't have to fight with any steps to get her son in or out of the house.

When they got inside, Amanda saw that the house had been vacuumed and cleaned since she left it two weeks ago. She never left a really messy house, but there wasn't any packaging remains from the medical equipment that had been delivered except for the paperwork that was on the table. They went to the bathroom, where Amanda inspected the shower head and the chair that was in the tub already. Jacob looked in from the hall, interested in seeing what they would use to give him a shower later.

They went to the boys' room, where Amanda found the biggest surprise of all. She had expected to find beds in the middle of the room with boxes on them and the whole room looking like it had only been painted, just as it did nearly two weeks earlier when she left. She found the boys' beds put together with sheets on them; beds made. The dresser drawers were against the wall with clothes put away. The box of trophies from soccer and basketball were sitting on a shelf on the wall. The little TV the boys owned, was already set up and ready to use. The whole room was ready for Jacob and Jackson. It couldn't have been more perfect. Amanda felt so relieved that she wouldn't have to deal with that project.

Amanda hugged Zachery, Eddy, and other family members that had helped get all the medical equipment set up and the room put together. For the next two hours or so, Amanda tried to relax and enjoy the fact that she was home and surrounded by family and friends again.

Chapter 25
Disguised Blessing

When it was just Eddy, Zachery, and Granny at the house, Amanda asked if they would be willing to sit with her kids for 20 minutes while she went to the store. She had already changed a diaper for Jacob, and realized she needed a few things to keep the toilet seat and diapers inconspicuous to everyone else. She knew it was embarrassing to Jacob, and the boys had to sleep in the room she was using to take care of Jacob's needs. She needed to get some cleaning supplies.

They agreed so she went to the store and bought disinfecting wipes, a diaper pail, extra gloves, scented cleaning sprays, and a box to keep the supplies in that would fit under the bed. She would try to make this experience as bearable as possible for everyone.

After she had returned, the rest of her family went home. Now it was just Amanda, Jacob, and Ally at home. Amanda started to think about what she would do for dinner.

"Mom, can I have a shower please?" Jacob asked. He was trying to push himself with his arms, but he wasn't able to use his left arm much, so he wasn't going anywhere.

"Yes, sweetie, we can do that," Amanda said, closing the pantry door. "I will need to start dinner as soon as we are done."

Amanda got behind Jacob and went back down the hall to his bedroom. Amanda got a movie started for Ally, so she would be occupied while she tried to give Jacob a bath. Amanda then grabbed some clean clothes for Jacob and went toward the bathroom, but just as she tried to go through the door, the wheelchair suddenly stopped. Since his chair had fit through all the other doors, she assumed it would fit through this one, but the bathroom door was just a couple inches too narrow for the chair. Amanda pushed a couple more times as if she just wasn't seeing things correctly. When it was obvious she wasn't going to get the chair in the door, Amanda fell on the floor and wept.

She had reached a breaking point. She wasn't exactly sure why. Maybe it was the stress she was feeling about their situation. Maybe it was that she hadn't seen this detail, and now she worried that she wasn't really prepared to take care of her son at home. Or maybe it was the fact that the bathroom was now inaccessible to her son, meaning he couldn't shower. Whatever it was, she just couldn't handle it, and she wanted to cry.

"Mom, don't cry," Jacob said, turning as best he could to look at his mother. He felt bad that she was breaking down now, but he couldn't do anything about it. "It's OK, Mom."

Amanda cried in silence for a few more minutes, and then stood up and said, "I'm sorry, Son. The slide board isn't that long, and I don't think it would be good for me to try and carry you the whole way. We will look into getting another wheelchair that will fit in this door."

Right about then, a knock came at the door. It was Amber, and she had a hot meal in her hands.

"Hey, welcome home," Amber began to say but noticed the redness in Amanda's face. She quickly asked, "What's wrong?"

"I'm being a baby about something dumb," Amanda said, not sure how that little episode would look to Amber, who had done a lot to help her get much of the medical equipment set up in her house.

"Well tell me what it is," Amber said, putting her free arm around Amanda. "Maybe I can help."

"Jacob really wanted to take a shower," Amanda explained, as they walked back toward the bathroom. "But when I went to push him into the bathroom, the wheelchair is too wide for the door."

"That's not silly at all," Amber said immediately. "That's a real problem. We will have to look into getting another wheelchair as soon as possible. But it will be a couple days at the earliest. Do you have another chair you can put in the bathroom that you can roll or drag on the linoleum?"

"We could use one of the kitchen chairs," Amanda said, considering the idea. "I'll try that."

"We will have to look into one of those electric wheelchairs," Amber said, as she was walking toward the front door. I know it's an added expense, but I will look for a program or something that will make it more affordable."

"Thank you for bringing dinner," Amanda said, as she took it to the kitchen counter. Amber and Amanda talked briefly about the medical equipment, then Amber said goodbye. Amanda wasn't really excited about buying another wheelchair. Jacob needed a way into the shower, and an electric chair would help him get around on his own.

Amanda got one of their kitchen chairs and put it just inside the door frame next to the wheelchair. Using the slide board, she transferred Jacob to the kitchen chair. Then she pushed the chair and Jacob to the edge of the tub; close enough to move him onto the shower chair. Seeing that the curtain would be in the way, Amanda put towels down on the floor by her and gave her son a shower. She got a little wet, and the floor got wet, but Jacob got the shower he needed. Amanda felt better because they were surviving.

After Jacob was dressed and in his wheelchair again, Amanda called her friend, Barbara. She often acted as a go-between when dropping off and picking up kids for Amanda and her ex-husband. Jackson had just been brought to Barbara's house, and she then brought Jackson to Amanda. When Jackson arrived, Amanda was thrilled to have everyone back together again. They ate dinner and talked about all that had gone on while she was in the hospital with Jacob.

Later that night, a storm rolled in, and it was raining heavily. Amanda had just laid down from turning Jacob again in his bed. Amanda had put a baby monitor in her bedroom so that if Jacob needed her, she would be able to reach him quickly. He hadn't gone more than 30 minutes over the past two hours without complaining that he was uncomfortable and needed to be moved. Amanda was sure she would fall asleep as soon as her head hit the pillow.

"What!!!" Amanda cried, as she picked her head up. Her pillow was wet. How could my pillow be wet? Amanda asked herself. She turned the light on and inspected her pillow, it was more than just a little damp. Nothing could have been spilled on it. Then the sound of rain outside made her look up. There was a wet spot on the ceiling. She saw another drop fall on her pillow.

Amanda closed her door and started a conversation with God.

"Do I need to be in a nuthouse?" she prayed aloud. She did get quite loud at times. "I don't know why this had to happen, but I can't take much more of this. I need a break. ... I need a lot of help and more strength than I have apparently. I don't have money to fix a roof. Why wasn't that seen when I got the inspection on the house? ... I hope you are getting a good laugh from all this, but for the record, I don't find this funny."

It was quiet in her room for a few minutes. Amanda tried to slow her pulse by taking a deep breath. She pulled her knees up and rested her head on them. In the back of her mind, she felt bad for the way she was talking, but she was at her wit's end. Amanda moved her bed, dried her pillow, and she spent the night on the couch.

The next day, Amanda called her home insurance company and opened a claim. She arranged for a builder to come and give her a quote to fix the roof. It was another day before the insurance adjuster came to look at the roof, and saw the quote for the repair. He looked around. He saw Amanda's bloodshot eyes from lack of sleep and crying. He saw the child in a wheelchair and the hospital equipment. He handed Amanda a check for more than the quoted price to fix the roof. Amanda looked at him confused.

"I hope this helps you get back on your feet," the adjuster

said. "Have a good day, ma'am."

He walked out, and Amanda leaned against the closed door. One tear rolled down the side of her face. She looked at the check again. She realized it was exactly enough to pay her mortgage for three more months. She felt a weight lifted from her shoulders. God had made it possible not only to fix the roof but provide a little more to help her through the months when she would not be able to work.

Amanda slid along the door and dropped to the floor. She said another prayer for gratitude and forgiveness. She would try to not complain anymore. God had shown His hand many times so far. He would help her again when she needed it. He was probably already making arrangements to address needs she would discover days and weeks from now. She knew that now.

Chapter 26
New Wheels

While the roof was being fixed on Saturday morning, Jacob was sitting in his wheelchair in the living room. Jackson almost brought out a tractor to play with but decided he would just play with cars instead. He grabbed four cars and made sure he had Jacob's favorite - a black truck.

Jackson walked into the living room and showed the cars to Jacob.

"Do you want to play with me, brother?" Jackson asked. He held out the black truck.

"How would I do that?" Jacob said, with a bite in his voice. "I can't get down on the floor."

"Oh, yeah," Jackson replied, trying to think about how they could still play cars. "I could push you to the table. We can play up there."

"Okay," Jacob said, not sure he really wanted to play cars anyway.

Jackson pushed Jacob to the table, but there were a bunch of papers on the table. Jacob wasn't sure what they were, but he knew Mom was looking at them. Jacob and Jackson just moved them to the side and started driving their cars around. Normally, this would have been enough to keep Jacob and Jackson going for hours, but after only 15 minutes, Jacob decided he wasn't interested in playing with cars anymore. When Jackson asked him why, Jacob got upset and yelled at him. Amanda heard this last part and came over to the boys.

"What's wrong, Jacob?" she asked. "It's not like you to not want to play with Jackson. Are you in pain?"

"Yeah, I'm hurting a little," Jacob said, not looking up. He knew he was acting strange, but he wasn't completely sure why.

"I bet you're tired too," Amanda said as she went to get the ibuprofen. "Neither one of us is getting much sleep with you needing to move every 45 minutes during the night."

"I am tired," Jacob said, taking the ibuprofen. "Can I lay down?"

Amanda looked at Jackson and could tell by his body language that he was sad. Amanda took Jacob to the bedroom to lay him down. Jackson followed behind slowly. As Amanda positioned Jacob on his left side facing the wall, she said, "I wish we had a better view for you. It seems that you either have the wall or the bottom of the bed to look at most of the time."

Jacob didn't respond.

Amanda then brought Jackson back out into the living room to talk with him.

"Why doesn't he want to play with me?" Jackson asked, when Amanda asked what was bothering him. "We used to always play together, but since he got home, I have tried to play with him, and he either gets upset or doesn't want to play very long."

Jackson hung his head.

"Jacob is in a lot of pain still," Amanda began. She pulled Jackson in close to her as she spoke to him. "He is also tired. He may be laying down a lot, but he doesn't get very much deep sleep because of the pain. Being cooped up in that chair or in bed all the time doesn't help. I'm sure he wishes he could run and play with you, but knowing he can't makes him feel bad."

Jackson looked into Amanda's face, but he wasn't cheering up.

"Just keep trying to help him have fun like you have been doing," Amanda concluded. "He will get better, and he'll have more energy to play soon."

Just after lunch, the repairs were done with the roof, and Amanda paid the contractor. After he left, Amanda started to go through her mail and saw all the bills that had come. She would have to contact her ex-husband and see if the insurance on his farm would help pay for the hospital bills. She wasn't excited about making that call. Seeing the debt mounting up, and knowing more would be coming, Amanda thought she should call Amber and tell her to forget about the electric wheelchair. She simply couldn't afford it.

Before she had a chance to call, there was a knock on the door. It was Amber, she had a big smile on her face.

"I have an electric wheelchair for you," Amber said and ran back to her truck where her husband was unloading it.

Amanda started to say, "But we can't ..."

Amber was already walking away, so Amanda followed her outside.

Amanda watched for a few minutes and then decided to say what needed to be said.

"Amber, I really appreciate what you've done, but we can't afford this," Amanda began. "I already don't know how I'm going to pay for everything else, and I won't ask you to foot the bill. We need to get this returned if possible."

"Oh, well I don't think that will be possible," Amber said, concern on her face, but not about the electric wheelchair. She was just concerned about her friend's situation. Amber's expression brightened, and she said, "I told a friend who goes to church with us about Jacob and all the medical equipment you had to buy and that you might need a wheelchair. After we talked, she said her grandma had an electric wheelchair she didn't need anymore since her husband recently passed away.

"Later that day, my friend called me back and said we could have it if we could come get it," Amber continued. "We went over and picked it up today, and here it is. It's free and works great. It should fit through the bathroom door and even turn around in there."

Amanda didn't know what to say. She was too overcome with joy and gratitude. Amanda gave Amber a smile as a tear well up in Amanda's eye. Amber smiled back and embraced her friend.

"And I brought you this," Amber said as she went to the cab of the truck. She pulled out a long body pillow.

"Oh, I don't need one of those," Amanda said, a little surprised at the gesture.

"Actually, I didn't get it for you," Amber said with a smile. "I got it for Jacob. You can use it behind him and in front of him or under him. It will just help him to be comfortable at night while he is recovering. The hospitals use a few pillows to achieve the same thing or a bed that changes position. I find these body pillows work pretty well at home."

Amanda was overcome by the thoughtfulness of her friend. She couldn't speak, so they just hugged again. Then Amanda drove the chair up the ramp and into the house. She tested out some of the features, many of which Amber had to show her. The seat could turn, the arm could be lifted for easy transfer, and the chair could even do a tight circle that made it possible for the chair to back right up to the tub. It was perfect.

They talked animatedly enough that Jacob called out wanting to get up to find out what was going on. Amanda was happy Amber would get to see Jacob's reaction.

Amanda got Jacob into his wheelchair and pushed him down the hall. His eyes widened in surprise when he saw the electric wheelchair. He was anxious to try it out. Amber helped to move Jacob into the new electric wheelchair. It didn't take long before Jacob was speeding around the house.

"This thing can go," Jacob said as he sped past Amanda, Amber, and her husband. They adults laughed. Jackson ran behind his brother, excited that his brother was so happy. Jackson opened the door and Jacob drove out the door and down the ramp. The two boys played outside for a while. Jacob was enjoying his new freedom.

Chapter 27
Doctor's Orders

Sunday was good. Amanda hadn't slept well since she had to move Jacob constantly during the night. Julie, a friend from the Pokeno group, had come to sit with the kids so Amanda could get a little nap. It had been a great thing for her. The Ratleys had come by and given her some money that members of the congregation had donated to help Amanda and her family. Amanda let them know that she was putting all the money she received into a separate bank account she would draw on for medical expenses. She really appreciated their support.

Julie had left them food for dinner which they ate together like many Sunday dinners before. It was sunset; Jacob, Jackson, and Ally were playing outside with Jacob's electric wheelchair. Amanda sat on a swing that hung from a huge oak tree in the front yard. It was a tranquil moment when she could just breathe and enjoy watching her kids play. As much as she wanted to stay focused on the simplicity in front of her, Amanda couldn't help thinking about the coming week and what she needed to do. She had to get the kids ready for going to school next week. She needed to work with the school board to get Jacob on the homebound program until Jacob could return to normal school. Then there was seeing if Jacob's dad's farm insurance would cover the medical expenses for the injury that happened on the farm. They would need to go back to Little Rock for follow-up appointments to make sure the bones were healing properly, and everything looked good.

On Friday her old employer had called Amanda to see if she was going to come back to work and when. Amanda felt pressured to say something, but couldn't answer that question then. She still didn't know what to say. Until Jacob was back at school, Amanda couldn't work full-time anywhere. Could she do part time before then? She didn't know. Right now she couldn't give her employer an answer, but inside she felt like she needed to do something else. Now wasn't the time to figure all that out, but she would have to address it soon.

So much to do.

Amanda continued to swing.

It was like the Sundays before the tractor incident. She would deal with those things tomorrow. Today, she needed the break from her problems and to just enjoy her kids. She wanted to celebrate the miracle of having Jacob alive rather than slog through the problems of life. They would be there tomorrow, and she would face them then. Today she would focus on the miracle of life and breathe.

Amanda looked at the kids and smiled. They were all touched by this experience. When Amanda went to lay Jacob down for a nap, Jacob found a new picture hung on the wall, and one taped to the bottom of the top bunk. They were drawn and hung by Jackson. He didn't say anything about it to Amanda. He just did it. Amanda also saw Jackson studying his Bible in the evening and praying frequently. She didn't have to encourage him. He was being the positive example for her. She loved it.

Jacob was always a good kid, but his prayers were more sincere since the incident. He was frustrated and sometimes short with them, but Amanda thought that was to be expected while he was recovering. Still, there were times when Jacob would tell Jackson that he loved him. Jacob had called Jackson in that afternoon when he first saw the pictures Jackson hung up for him and said he really liked them. Amanda knew they were working things out in their own way.

As she watched them chase Jacob on his electric

wheelchair, Amanda said to herself, *I certainly don't want to go through this again. But I can't deny that God is doing good things in our lives.*

Monday did come, and Amanda began working on the problems that hung over her the day before. First was the school problem. Amanda's dad sat with Jacob, Jackson, and Ally, while she went to visit with Ms. La Roe, who was over the homebound program at the school. Ms. La Roe didn't think Jacob was a candidate for the program. Amanda assured her he was and explained what the hospital teacher at Arkansas Children's Hospital said. Ms. La Roe wasn't convinced and said that the hospital teacher doesn't know Louisiana regulations. Amanda was sure the hospital teacher had done her research, but Amanda knew she would have to spell it out for Ms. La Roe. Amanda told Ms. La Roe that she had talked with a cousin who was working on her master degree in education in Baton Rouge, and her teachers were on the state education board. They were telling her Jacob was a perfect candidate for the program. Ms. La Roe wanted to see it in writing.

"I will get it in writing," Amanda said. "I would appreciate it if you would start working on finding a teacher and make preparations, so Jacob doesn't get behind due to paperwork."

"I can't do much until we know he will be able to use the program," replied Ms. La Roe, with a half smile.

It was really quite simple. The homebound program required the school to provide school work that Jacob could do at home. They had to provide a teacher to come to Amanda's house twice a week for two hours to go over his work and help teach concepts that Jacob didn't understand. The school would have to pay for the teacher and coordinate with Jacob's usual teachers to get his school work. Amanda was sure the extra cost and coordination were the hang-up. It would only be in place until Jacob could go to school and function like normal without excessive pain. Until then, Jackson or Amanda would pick up Jacob's school work at the end of each school day and turn in work from the previous day. Amanda hoped it would work well enough that Jacob wouldn't be too far behind.

When Amanda got home, she called her cousin and relayed her conversation with the school. Her cousin sent her an email with links to find the regulations and what pages to bring to the school. Amanda spent a few hours reading about the program and what it officially said. She printed out many pages and marked the important parts for their situation.

At one point, when she had to take a break from her research to take care of Jacob, he was excited to show Amanda what grandpa had done. Amanda's dad had figured out a way to attach a 2x4 board to the bottom of the top bunk bed. Then he attached two tan, nylon armbands to the board. The bands had been used to hold Jacob down at the hospital. Now the bands were hanging above Jacob so that he could use it to help him move and sit up. At first, Jacob only used his right arm. Eventually, Jacob figured he could use it to help his left arm get stronger.

Early the next day, Amanda went to see Ms. La Roe. Amanda handed her 15 pages of information about the program and who it served. Amanda had underlined and highlighted the parts that pertained to her situation. Ms. La Roe wasn't smiling this time. Amanda also shared an email that her cousin sent from her teacher that was on the state's education board, explaining what was intended when the program was created. Ms. La Roe agreed that she had misunderstood and would start working on making arrangements for Jacob. As Amanda was leaving, Ms. La Roe said these things could take time. Amanda thanked her for her efforts and would share the same information with the superintendent, so he could help with any hurdles that might come up. Ms. La Roe walked away quickly.

Amanda contacted Arkansas Children's Hospital after her visit with the school representative. The hospital said they would get all the paperwork in order before her appointment on Thursday.

Next Amanda contacted her ex-husband to see if he was

going to make a claim on his farm insurance to help with the bills. He said he didn't have insurance and couldn't help. Amanda knew better than that. She had kept his finances for many years and knew he had insurance. She would have to find out on her own. Amanda sighed; more work.

On Wednesday, Amanda spent some time with Jackson to make sure he was ready for school. His father had taken him shopping for new clothes and got him a new backpack. Ally was not yet in kindergarten so she would stay home with Amanda until Jacob could go to school and she could get a job.

Before Amanda knew it, it was Thursday, and she was driving back to Little Rock for Jacob to see the doctor. It was a long three-hour drive. Jacob complained many times during the trip that he was uncomfortable. At home, Jacob had many options for moving and getting comfortable. In the car, he was restricted by the seatbelt. Amanda tried to talk to Jacob to help keep his mind off his discomfort.

At the doctor's clinic, the physicians took an x-ray of Jacob's pelvic bone. The doctor said Jacob was healing well, and they could schedule physical therapy.

"We will see you again next week," the doctor said. "We will schedule another visit two weeks after that."

"How is his arm healing?" Amanda asked the doctor. "Can he start moving it and trying to use it?"

"It's been almost three weeks," the doctor said after consulting Jacob's records. "I think he can start trying to lift it, but he shouldn't try to pick up anything with it. The physical therapist will give you exercises that will help him get his range of motion back and his strength in due time."

"How often should we schedule physical therapy visits?" Amanda asked.

"Generally, they schedule visits twice a week," the doctor said. "Sometimes less or sometimes more depending on the injury and needs. It also depends on how sore Jacob gets after therapy. The important thing is to be consistent and diligent with what the therapist tells you to do at home. The work you do between visits is as important as the visits themselves."

On the way home, Jacob tried to lift his arm. The thought of getting his left arm back was exciting at first, but after nearly three weeks of not using it, his arm was not very responsive, and it hurt to use it. Amanda saw the discouragement in Jacob's face.

"It will take time to get full use of your arm," she began. "We will get the physical therapy started next week so you can start using your arm again in no time. You'll probably have to work really hard to get better by hunting season."

That perked him up. Jacob spent much of the next three hours working on lifting his arm a few inches off the seat. At first, he was frustrated and constantly uncomfortable. These feelings gave way to a desire to work and get better so he could pull himself up into a deer blind. The pain was bearable with a goal in site, however far away it was.

Chapter 28
Range of Motion

Jackson and Ally spent the weekend with their father. Amanda tried to get a couple naps when Jacob was sleeping. It helped her to feel more like a person and less like a zombie. She was really glad to have her kids back on Sunday evening though. She got the kids bathed and ready for bed. Jackson was excited about school. Jacob talked like he was happy not to go to school, but Amanda thought it sounded like he was trying to convince himself.

"You mean you aren't ready to get back to school?" Amanda asked again, hoping he would be more truthful about his thoughts.

"I'm not excited about going to school," Jacob said. "I don't know anyone that is."

"What about seeing your friends?" Amanda asked.

He paused, then answered, "Yeah, I would like to see my friends and talk to them again."

That night at 11:00 pm, the boys had been asleep for an hour and a half at least, when Amanda heard yelling coming from the boys' room. She ran down the hall to see what was wrong. Jackson was sitting up, yelling, "Stop! Stop! You've run over my brother!"

Amanda wrapped him in her arms. He clung to her and cried.

"What's wrong with Brother?" Jacob asked, who had been awakened by the screaming, too.

"It sounds like he was having a bad dream," Amanda offered.

"I dreamed that Jacob was run over again," Jackson said through the sobs. "This time the plow went over him and cut him up bad."

Amanda gasped at the mental image, and said, "That must have been awful! It's okay now. You are safe at home, and so is Jacob."

Amanda held onto Jackson for ten minutes as he calmed down and eventually went back to sleep. She wondered if it was riding in the truck again, or if his dad talked about the tractor incident to Jackson. She was glad they were safe at home, and she prayed that Jackson's dream wouldn't be a reality.

The next morning, Jackson seemed to be fine again and ready to go to school. It was the second Monday in August and the first day of school. Jacob watched his brother leave. He didn't like being left behind. He rode his electric wheelchair to the end of the driveway and watched as Amanda walked Jackson across the street. Jackson went the rest of the way to the school on his own, while Jacob and Amanda watched him almost all the way to the doors. Jacob hoped he would be back at school soon, even if he had to go to school in a wheelchair.

There was no time frame for when Jacob would return to regular school. Right now Jacob needed Tylenol or Ibuprofen regularly. School policy was that kids couldn't bring medication to school so they would have to figure out that hurdle before Jacob could go to school. He was still not sleeping well during the night, and neither was she because he needed her help moving to get comfortable. He was making progress though. There were times he would move himself a little with his right arm, so he didn't have to wake Amanda. But he still just didn't have the mobility to move much without her.

Jacob watched the clock most of that day. He had a hard time playing with Jackson like they used to because the games and toys were either on the floor, or required movements that Jacob found difficult now. It frustrated Jacob, and so many times he was short with Jackson. Now that Jackson wasn't there, Jacob missed his brother. Ten minutes before the end of school, Jacob drove his electric wheelchair out the side door and waited for his brother. Amanda saw Jacob go out and recognized what was going on. She knew that therapy and school would be helpful for Jacob, and he wouldn't have to wait much longer. Since they got the green light at their last doctor's appointment, Amanda set up a physical therapy session the next afternoon. It was an hour drive one way to the physical therapist, and they would see him twice a week.

Amanda looked at her week. On Tuesday and Thursday, they were going to the rehab center near Monroe, Louisiana, for physical therapy. Then on Wednesday, they would go to the doctors in Little Rock for a follow-up visit. She would spend more than 10 hours in the car over those three days, plus all the unloading and loading and time at appointments. She would be busy. But thanks to her church and other churches in the area, she at least had some gas money to make those appointments. She just had to help Jacob get better.

When Jackson got home from school, he looked sad and stressed. Amanda asked him what was wrong.

"It seemed like everyone, including the teachers, wanted to know what happened," he said, nearly starting to cry. "I almost started to tell the first person, but when others began to gather around, and I started to think about what I saw, I walked away. I just walked away from anyone that asked about Jacob getting run over. I don't know how to handle it."

"I think you handled it pretty well, Jackson," Amanda said, pulling him in to give him a hug. "It was a horrible thing to see, and you don't have to tell anyone about it. I think it would be better not to talk about it actually. The pain is still too fresh. So either walk away or tell them you aren't ready to talk about it yet and change the subject."

Jackson said he would do that and went to play with his brother.

On Tuesday, after Jackson got off to school, Amanda

took Ally to a babysitter, and then she took Jacob to see the physical therapist. Jacob was excited to get started with working to get better. He wasn't sure what they would do, but Jacob had already worked at raising his arm almost a foot on his own. It hurt a lot, so he didn't work at it often, but maybe the physical therapist would help him know what to expect.

When they got to the clinic, Amanda went to get Jacob out of the car. She had moved him many times every day since they were home. She thought she was getting stronger and it would get easier. But this time, she felt a pinch in her back as she tried to lift Jacob onto the slide board. When she cried out in pain, Jacob looked worriedly at her. Amanda finished moving him to his chair and then grabbed her lower back.

"I'm sorry Momma," Jacob said.

"Don't you be sorry about anything," Amanda said resolutely. "I'd rather have a back hurting from moving you in and out of cars, than from putting flowers on a grave."

Amanda pushed Jacob into the clinic. After signing in, they met an energetic, happy man that introduced himself as Lon. He was thin, had light brown hair and a broad smile. He would be their therapist.

"I've heard a little about your accident," Lon said to Jacob. "You have to be one of the toughest people I know. I want to help you get back on your feet, OK?"

"OK," Jacob said with a smile.

"First, let me tell you a little about how this works and what you will need to do to get better," Lon continued. "Most importantly, you need to listen to your body. If you hurt a lot, tell me. A little soreness is fine because that means we are doing something. If you are hurting a lot, we could be making things worse. I need you to tell me though, OK?"

"OK," Jacob replied.

"What we do here will be learning exercises and stretches, but you have to keep working at it at home," Lon continued. "We will not make the progress we want if you don't do the stretches and exercises between appointments, got it?"

"Got it," Jacob answered.

"Alright, so you are only three weeks from your surgery when you got that fancy hardware in your hip," Lon said. "We can't do weight exercise until six weeks, but before we do that we need to stretch your muscles and move your legs. That goes for your arm too. So let's get you up on this table, and we will start with some movement. I will do all the moving, you just need to relax."

Lon helped Amanda move Jacob onto the table. Amanda was happy to let Lon do most of the lifting so she could save her back for later. Jacob remembered Amanda's back pain once he was sitting on the table.

"Maybe you can help my mom too, while we are here," Jacob said to Lon, but he was looking at his mom. She was a little surprised by what Jacob said. "She's hurt her back lugging me around. Maybe she needs to learn some stretches."

"Sure, we can help with that," Lon said, the understanding flooding to his mind. "You will be critical to his recovery, so we can go over a few things when we are done with Jacob, OK?"

"I'm fine," Amanda said, putting her arm around Jacob. "Let's get him back to walking, and my back will get better pretty quick."

Lon helped Jacob lay down on the table, then he showed Amanda how to support his right leg and move it slowly to the sides and then up and down. All the while, Lon was asking Jacob to let him know when it was starting to hurt. They did the same thing with his left leg. Lon explained a couple other stretches that they should do at home. He suggested they do each exercise and stretch five times. They would see how Jacob was feeling Thursday and then determine if they could increase the repetitions.

In order to strengthen Jacob's core, they sat Jacob up and put a ball two feet off to the side of Jacob. Then with Lon there to help steady Jacob, Lon asked him to lean over and pick up the ball. This simple exercise was surprisingly difficult for Jacob at first. Jacob's injuries and immobility had left his core muscles weak. Simply leaning over required him to engage his abdominal and back muscles. Lon repeated the exercise to the other side and to the front. Lon explained to Amanda how to do the exercises at home and how to support Jacob. Lon explained to Amanda how to do the exercises at home and how to support Jacob. Then Lon showed her a couple of things she could do to make the exercise slightly more challenging, once Jacob got more comfortable with it.

When they moved on to Jacob's arm, Jacob explained that he was trying to lift his arm and could raise it a foot above his legs. Lon was impressed but said they would work on stretches and range of motion for a week or so and then work on building the muscle control. So Lon took Jacob's left arm and raised it for him to the front until Jacob said it started to hurt. Then they did the same thing to the side, raising his arm up until Jacob said it hurt.

"Very good," Lon said. "We will do this a few more times, and then I will have your mom go through all the exercises again so we can be sure you will get your stretches done at home. Don't get discouraged that we aren't doing more strengthening right now. It' important to stretch and get the muscles loose first. If we bind them up, you may lose some range of motion."

True to his word, once they were through with Jacob's stretches, Lon gave Amanda some pointers on stretches and exercises she could do to strengthen her core and keep herself healthy until Jacob could help out more with the moving.

On the way home, Jacob spent some time moving his arm out and then up. He couldn't lift his arm very much, but he wanted to help the repaired muscles stretch a little. He was anxious to do what Lon had told him so he could get back to normal quickly. Meanwhile, Amanda decided that she did need to take the time to strengthen her body. She decided she would go for a short run every day as well as the exercises she learned at the clinic. They would both get stronger from this experience.

Chapter 29
Hydro Therapy

The next day Amanda and Jacob had their second follow-up appointment with the orthopedic doctors in Little Rock. After getting Jackson to school, they started the day with exercises and stretching for Amanda and Jacob. Then Amanda loaded up Ally and Jacob and took Ally to a babysitter and started north for Little Rock.

Amanda didn't like these visits to Little Rock very much. It was a long trip, and she knew it was uncomfortable for Jacob to sit still that long. For Amanda, it also meant most of her day was spent going to the doctor's office. She knew the care he would receive would be great, but when it was all said and done, she spent more than nine hours going to the doctor. She had six hours of driving, three hours in the doctor's office with waiting, x-rays, waiting some more, and seeing the doctor. Sometimes they would have to make stops along the way. She had to coordinate with family and friends to get Jackson picked up from school and sometimes even Ally from the babysitter. So even though Amanda really only got one thing done, the day seemed to be busy, hectic, and rather unproductive.

I'm glad we will only be doing three more of these visits, Amanda thought to herself as she drove north on Highway 65. *August is almost a third of the way through and I feel like I've been running a million miles an hour, but when I think about what I've accomplished, it's just been taking care of Jacob.*

"Mom, my back hurts," Jacob said from the back seat. He was pushing his right arm behind his back to try and make the ache go away.

"I'm sorry, Jacob," Amanda replied, looking at him in the rearview mirror. "I can't really give you anything else. And we can't really stop unless it's an emergency 'cause we might be late if we do. Can you shift your position a little?"

"I'll try," was Jacob's response. He had already tried shifting, and it helped for 10 minutes. The pain was already a little better since pushing his fist behind his lower back. He would rather just keep going than stop and have his Mom try to move him.

They made it to the clinic and met with the orthopedic doctor. Everything looked good with Jacob's recovery, and the doctor encouraged them to continue to keep doing what they were doing.

"The scars seem to be healing really well," the physician said as he looked at the place where they opened the skin to put in the 12-inch metal plate. "It's almost been four weeks since the operation, so you don't have to worry about submerging him. I'm sure you have noticed that you don't have to worry about drying his skin lately since most of the tissue is closed and healed nicely."

"Does that mean I can have a bath?" Jacob asked.

"I think we will still do the showers on the chair," Amanda said. "It's hard enough moving you to the chair and back when you are wet. It will be even harder to pick you up from the floor."

"Yeah, I would agree that baths are not advisable until you can stand on your own," the doctor added.

Amanda saw that Jacob was a little disappointed. She knew he liked to swim - especially on the hot days. Amanda wished she could take her kids swimming. It had been out of the question for the last four weeks, but now she wondered if Jacob could do a little swimming with support.

"Would it be okay for Jacob to be put in a swimming pool if we could lower him in safely?" Amanda asked. Then seeing the puzzled look on the doctor's face, she quickly added, "I would get in with him and hold him up of course. He would be lighter in the water, and it would help him with his flexibility."

"I think you would have the same problem in a pool as we just pointed out with a tub," the doctor began. "But you have a good point about the water therapy. It's called hydro therapy, and it will help with his range of motion and flexibility as well as muscle control. If you can do it safely, and the physical therapist can give you some exercises, I think it would be fine. Just be careful moving him in and out of the water and never leave him in the water alone."

"I won't," Amanda quickly added. She didn't need much prodding to connect the logical consequence of leaving a child with no use of his legs and limited use of his left arm in a pool alone. "It would only be for therapy. I wouldn't leave him to let him play."

Jacob was excited by this conversation. He thought water therapy sounded better than laying on a table. He missed swimming. This was the best news the doctor could have given him.

Jacob peppered Amanda with questions about when they would go swimming, and what they would do in the pool. He was trying to picture himself in the water, and how his mom would be able to hold him up. He knew that when she said she would do something she would find a way. He wanted to know what her plan was.

Amanda had to repeatedly tell Jacob she hadn't worked out all the details. They would first have to get some exercises from the physical therapist. Then she would have to see if a friend would let them use their pool.

"So before you go trying to put your swimsuit on, we need to work out a plan," Amanda said to Jacob. "We can't just show up at someone's house and start using their pool. We will ask the physical therapist tomorrow, and then we will see when we can get in a pool."

Jacob was content with that plan. He envisioned being in a pool by Friday. He busied himself with dreaming about swimming and asked more questions most of the way home. He hardly noticed the aches in his body for the excitement he felt.

Amanda picked up Jackson and Ally on her way home and then she made dinner. By the end of the day, Amanda felt drained though not exactly sure why. She still wasn't sleeping well, but the day of traveling and constant movement in her life right now was leaving her exhausted. Just as Amanda was about to crawl into bed at 11:15 pm, she heard Jacob call out. He needed to be cleaned up after relieving himself. With minimal light so she wouldn't wake up Jackson, Amanda gathered her materials and changed Jacob's diaper. Once he was cleaned, she got him situated in his bed. She disposed of the diaper, washed her hands, and put away the wipes and other supplies she had just used.

Finally, she was able to go to sleep after 11:30 pm. She knew she would be up in about an hour to help Jacob get comfortable. She started to think about what time it might be when he would call for her, but before she got very far in that thought process, she was already asleep.

Chapter 30

Sore Arms

Jacob was excited to go to physical therapy on Thursday, August 12. He couldn't wait to ask about the water exercises. He was also excited to show how much progress he was making with lifting his arm. The stretching had really helped. He was able to pick his arm up two feet from his lap. His arm was definitely sore, but it wasn't anything worse than the other pain he was feeling. Since the doctors said it was normal, this pain must be normal, too.

They got to physical therapy at 11:00 am. Jacob didn't even wait for Lon to ask him how he was feeling. He launched into 'show and tell' right after they said hello. Lon was clearly impressed.

"You are doing great," Lon said to Jacob as he took over pushing the wheelchair for Amanda. "I think you will like some of the new exercises we will show you today."

"Can you show us some water exercises?" Jacob quickly asked.

"I hadn't planned to," Lon said and then turned to Amanda.

"We talked to the orthopedic doctor yesterday, and he said Jacob can be submerged now," Amanda explained. Lon nodded as he listened, understanding coming quickly as Amanda talked. "Hydro therapy, I believe, is what he called it. Jacob is really excited about doing some water exercises. If you think he can do it, we would like you to show us some things we can try in a pool."

"Well, I think hydro therapy will be great, but I worry

most about how you would support him in the water," Lon explained. "We will go over a couple exercises, but first let's see if it's painful for Jacob to be held under the shoulders, particularly the left one."

They slid Jacob onto the table, just like they had started out the last session of therapy. Before Lon had Jacob lay down, he got behind Jacob and asked him to say "when" if it got painful.

Lon put his arms under Jacob's arms and around his chest. Then Lon lifted Jacob off the table six inches. Amanda was standing in front of Jacob and saw from his expression that it hurt him, but he didn't say anything. Lon set him down.

"How did that feel?" Lon asked. "Did it hurt under your left arm or anywhere else?"

Jacob hesitated and then admitted that it did hurt.

"I think if you work on moving the muscle around and keep stretching, it won't hurt too much to get picked up like that," Lon said to Jacob. "I can show your mom how to massage the scar so that it breaks up the scar tissue underneath, which will help with your flexibility and the sensitivity when you are picked up under the arms. I know you are excited about getting in a pool, but I think it would be helpful to wait a little longer before we put you in the water. Let's wait a week or two, OK?"

Jacob agreed, and they continued to work on some new stretches. Jacob was not as enthusiastic about his therapy that day, and Amanda noticed it. Amanda didn't like how painful the massaging was for Jacob, but she understood that it would be helpful. On their way home, Amanda tried to cheer up Jacob.

"Jacob, I know you want to go swimming," she began. "He didn't say we couldn't try it, we just don't want to hurt you in the process. We will work on stretches just like Lon said, and then when it doesn't hurt, we will get you in the pool."

"Yes, ma'am," Jacob said. His face showing he wasn't comforted much by her words, but wouldn't fight it anymore. Jacob started rubbing his left arm where the doctors fixed sewed it up nearly a month before. He didn't think he would ever be free from the pain. He was always in some discomfort, so what difference did it make to cause his arm to hurt a little. Jacob knew the folly of this argument as he made it. He rubbed his arm some more while he looked out the window.

When they got home, Jacob asked his mom if he could just go lay down for a little while.

"Jacob, we need to work on your school work," Amanda replied, as she pushed him up the ramp and into the house. "You don't have much, so it won't take long."

"Can I just rest for 30 minutes and then work on my school work?" Jacob asked.

Amanda didn't want him to sink into a dark depression on his own, but she also knew she needed breaks occasionally before continuing. She took him back to his room. Before she could lay him down on his bed, she had to change his diaper.

"This is so humiliating to be in diapers, mom," Jacob said. "Why can't I control it better? Why can't I start walking? Why can't I use my left arm more? Why did this happen?"

It was quiet for a few minutes as Amanda got Jacob cleaned up - both allowing the other to think.

"I don't know why this had to happen, but it did," Amanda said in a firm yet kind voice. "I have wondered why this happened too, but I don't think we will know why until we are all the way through this trial. The only thing I know is that we have been blessed, and this whole ordeal has shown us and others how much God is taking care of us. Bad things happen to everyone, but we can choose to look for the good or the bad. We will find what we are looking for."

Amanda paused, then continued, "You sound like you are disappointed with your progress. You are actually getting better really quickly. This time two weeks ago, you were just coming home from a long stay in the hospital. The week before that you were on a ventilator and in a coma.

Your progress may not be as fast as you would like, but it's actually a miracle that you are alive at all. So be patient with yourself and with God. I have been frustrated with God at times too, but I have also seen how some things that seem awful have helped us later.

"I'll let you have 30 minutes, and then I will come get you so you can start on your school work," Amanda said as she walked out of the room.

Jacob lay on his back and stared at the straps hanging above him. He was thinking about what his mom had said. He was getting better at doing things, and his arm was improving quickly. All the incisions from surgery were healing well and he was starting to sleep better at night. He briefly recalled Jackson's account of what happened and knew he was lucky to even be alive.

After five minutes of staring, Jacob decided to try and reach the strap with his left arm. He had been able to lift his arm up 45 degrees earlier. He would have to use his right arm to get his left arm to reach its destination. He lifted his left arm as far as he could, but couldn't quite get it to the strap. He still needed to raise his arm more than two feet to reach the it. He grabbed his left arm with his right hand and picked it up the rest of the way and grabbed the strap.

Jacob smiled to himself though his arm hurt from the exertion. He didn't try to pull himself up; he knew that would be too much. But he let his left arm hang straight up for a few minutes. Then he used his right arm to help control his left arm as he dropped it back down on the bed. He rested for a bit and then repeated the exercise again. After a third grab on the strap, Jacob decided he should rest. The effort left him breathing heavy, but he was happy.

Chapter 31
Homebound Program

The next day, Amanda's grandma came to sit with Jacob at noon so she could go to the school and double check that everything was set for the homebound program to start the following week. Amanda wasn't sure why it was such a hassle, but it had been a long drawn out dialog with the superintendent, the school board, and especially the woman that was over the program. Amanda wasn't sure if the woman didn't want to help or didn't understand the program, but Amanda had researched the Louisiana homebound program and had countless conversations with her cousin and others so she would know the program. Amanda then had to teach the school board about the program and what it should be used for. With all the negotiations over, Amanda hoped today would just be a confirmation that everything was in place for Jacob to start the next week.

"Hello, Ms. Brown," said the receptionist when Amanda walked in. "Are you here to pick up Jacob's school work?"

"If it's ready, yes," Amanda said with a smile. "I also need to visit with Ms. La Roe about the homebound program."

The receptionist's smile faded, but she said, she would let her know. Five minutes later, Ms. La Roe came out to see Amanda.

"Hello, Ms. La Roe," said Amanda, as pleasantly as she could. "I just wanted to come and double check that we are all set for next week with the homebound teacher."

"We are working on it," said Ms. La Roe. "It's not as

simple as you think. We have to find a teacher that is willing to take on the extra work, and the school has to approve the money to pay the teacher for the extra hours."

"I know it is a process," Amanda said, still maintaining a happy demeanor. "I know it's an additional expense, but as a taxpayer in Louisiana with a child that qualifies for the program, we are within our rights to have the added assistance until Jacob can return to school. We have been working on this for more than two weeks. You told me on August 2 that you should be able to get the teacher identified and scheduled to begin by August 16, which is Monday. Arkansas Children's Hospital reached out to you in July, so you have known about this for nearly a month. Will we have a teacher coming to our house next week?"

"We will try," was all Ms. La Roe would offer.

Amanda didn't like to push so hard, but she had known from the first conversation that she would have to be assertive to get this program going in her home. She hoped it would only be a month before Jacob could be back in school, but she didn't want to have him fall behind unnecessarily.

"Will you call me when you have a teacher selected?" Amanda said. "We have physical therapy on Tuesdays and Thursdays, and other appointments with doctors to work around, so I need to get her schedule as early as possible."

"I will call you as soon as we have a teacher," Ms. La Roe agreed. "I will talk to a few teachers today."

"Thank you," Amanda said and left the office.

Ms. La Roe did call around 4:00 pm that day. Amanda was helping Jacob with his stretches when the call came. Ms. La Roe said she had a teacher that would work with Jacob, but she could only do after school on Tuesdays and Thursdays. If that wouldn't work, then she would need a little more time to get another teacher. Amanda wasn't sure if that was a coincidence or a ploy, but she told Ms. La Roe that they would work with that. After a short pause, Ms. La Roe told her the name and to expect her around 2:45 pm on Tuesday. Amanda hoped the teacher was more excited to help than Ms. La Roe.

After an all-too-quick weekend, it was time for Jackson to start his second week of school. Jacob had no trouble with the first week of work since it was all a review. The work that Jackson brought home on Monday had a few concepts that were new to Jacob. They hoped the teacher that would come Tuesday would shed some light on the subjects.

Amanda and Jacob rushed home from physical therapy so they wouldn't be late for the homebound teacher. Ms. White showed up around 2:30 pm with less enthusiasm than a stubborn donkey. She spent a few minutes going over the work Jacob had completed and then tried to explain a few of the assignments that Jacob didn't understand. At 3:30 Ms. White said she had some things to do, so she had to leave early. Amanda was disappointed that the teacher wasn't doing what she had agreed to do, but Amanda didn't want to judge her. Maybe this was an anomaly, and she had some pressing business. Amanda worked with Jacob to try to clarify any other questions he had about his school work.

Thursday was a little better. Ms. White showed up on time but said she would have to leave again at 3:30 pm. She was a bit more helpful with Jacob's questions this time, which was good. His school work was getting more challenging because of the new material his classes were covering.

Today Amanda took advantage of the time when Ms. White was working with Jacob to go outside and relax. She had spent every waking moment changing diapers, picking up her 150-pound son to change seats, giving medicine, fixing food, cleaning up messes, paying bills, making phone calls, helping with homework, and taking care of Jackson and Ally. Amanda went outside to sit on the swing and breathe.

Jackson and Ally were playing together by the trees at the side of the house. Despite the heat outside, Amanda wanted to take a break from her responsibilities in the house. She didn't want to think about anything. She watched birds singing in the branches and felt the wind blowing as she sat on the swing in the big oak tree. She rubbed her shoulders and back as she relaxed. She remembered thinking about how two months before she thought life was going to slow down, and that she was getting a hold of things. Amanda laughed at her foolish prediction. Maybe someday it would come true, but not today and not for a long time. Amanda swung back and forth - quietly thinking.

The scariest part was that no one knew how long Jacob's recovery would take. Jacob's bones would heal, and his scars would close, but how long would the pain last? Would Jacob be walking in October, or would it take him until December? No one knew for sure. Jacob was working hard, and so far the recovery was going well (that's kind of what her life looked like two months ago - everything was fine until ...). She didn't know when the next surprise or setback would come.

Amanda breathed in and sighed. She wrapped her arms around herself in a personal hug, and a tear came to her eye. She had to be strong for everyone else, but when she had a chance to think about how she was doing, she realized this was taking a toll on her. The pressure of taking care of a handicapped child all of a sudden, the financial strain and uncertainty of their situation, and the emotional tension of doing it alone was harder than she would have believed possible.

Amanda wouldn't allow herself to think about all the negatives without at least acknowledging the grace she had experienced. She wasn't doing this alone. She actually did have people who had come to her aid, even before she had asked. In fact, most of them were in route before she even knew she needed the help. She was struggling with the physical burden, but she was able to endure more physical exertion than she ever had before. While she had no job, the charity of others had helped her stay afloat without getting behind on her living expenses and cover the traveling costs they were incurring. Surprisingly, Jacob wasn't having any signs of infection or setbacks from her care, despite the crash course she received in the hospital and inadequacies she felt. In her heart, Amanda knew Jacob was making a lot of progress in his recovery, which was a miracle in itself. Naturally, she had doubts and fears, but it was good for her to see them and match them with the power of God that had helped her overcome those problems.

At 3:30, Ms. White left, and Amanda squared her shoulders and resumed the load she had to bear. She enjoyed the break but was ready to get moving again. It helped her keep her thoughts in check.

Chapter 32
Pool Time

On Friday the 20th, Jackson and Ally went to their dad's house for the weekend. It looked like Amanda was going to get some quiet time with Jacob. At 6:00 pm, Amanda's former sister-in-law called and asked if she could take Jacob to her house to go fishing with his younger cousin tomorrow. She would keep a close eye on him, and they would have him back by lunch time. Amanda knew how much Jacob liked fishing. This aunt and uncle were very responsible, so Amanda wasn't worried about Jacob's safety with them. She consented and let Jacob know that his aunt would be there at 8:00 am to take him fishing. He got really excited about that, though he was a little concerned what would happen if he needed to be cleaned up. Amanda assured him that she wasn't far away and would come take care of him if he needed her.

As promised, Jacob's aunt came at 8:00 am. Amanda had just cleaned him up and got him ready to go when they arrived. Jacob was beaming with excitement. Amanda talked to them about transferring him to seats and got the push wheelchair loaded in their truck.

Amanda would have nearly four hours to herself so she began to think about all the things she wanted to accomplish. She sat down on the couch to make a list of what needed to be done. She only wrote down a few items before she gave up and took a nap. Two hours later, she woke up feeling refreshed and energized. She swept and mopped the kitchen floor and vacuumed the carpets. She started laundry and clipped her nails.

Then she sat down to take advantage of the quiet to think about her situation. It had been more than a month since Jacob was hospitalized. By now she thought she had all the bills for the doctors and hospital. On Friday she had received the first bill that told her what the Medicare insurance wouldn't cover. It totaled more than $75,000. She was in shock when she saw the number and just put it down - not wanting to think about it anymore. She remembered it now though, and she knew she had to push to get help from Jacob's dad - more specifically the insurance company that covered the farm in this kind of incident. Jacob's dad had given her no information and flat-out refused to make a claim. Amanda had found out what insurance company covered the farm and let her lawyer know about her financial situation. They discussed how they could contact the insurance company about getting help paying bills and getting a settlement. It wouldn't be a quick resolution, but there was a flicker of hope on the horizon that she wouldn't be stuck paying for a second debt that was practically a second mortgage. There was no job to pay either debt off. Jacob wasn't even done with the recovery. There would be more bills to pay. As excited as Amanda had been at getting this brief break, the silence was not turning out to be that soothing. Amanda decided to go soak in the bath for a while before Jacob came home.

Jacob arrived home around noon and was excited to tell Amanda all about his experience. As she made lunch, he sat in his wheelchair next to her and talked.

"We had a great time fishing in their pond," Jacob began, his cheeks pink from being outside. "We fished until all the worms were gone, then Billy started using raisins to bait his hook. The crazy thing is it worked. He pulled out a 15-inch white perch. I've never seen anything like that."

"I've never seen anyone use a raisin to fish either," Amanda asked in disbelief. "That's too funny."

"Yeah, it was huge," Jacob replied. Then he paused, thinking back over the day. "Momma, I felt normal again. It was just cousins fishing. The smell of the grass and seeing the trees. We sat there like we used to in camping chairs and it felt normal."

Amanda looked at the happy expression on Jacob's face and smiled. She was grateful that such a simple experience could bring him joy and that his aunt invited him to do something he loved. Jacob had been able to go and feel normal again. He had been dealing with the reality of the pain for so long that he probably didn't think it would ever go away. His young mind was consumed with the limitations that he was losing hope of being normal. Amanda could see that this experience gave Jacob a boost she couldn't give him. He was invigorated with a taste of life after the recovery.

Thank God for that, Amanda thought. *He is still working His miracle.*

Later that day, Amanda was looking at hotels in Little Rock. Jacob's next doctor's appointment was scheduled for 8:00 am on Wednesday, and with a long drive before hand, they would need to travel up to Little Rock on Tuesday night. As Amanda looked at hotels, Jacob drove up in his electric wheelchair. There happened to be a picture of a pool showing on the hotel's website when he arrived.

"Can we stay in that one, Momma?" Jacob asked. "I'm sure my shoulder won't hurt now. Let's try it, please."

"I was thinking of staying in that hotel anyway," Amanda said, as she started to look through the amenities. "It actually has a handicap accessible pool. I think that means it has a lift chair to help put you in the water. We can get some water exercises on Tuesday at physical therapy and then drive up to Little Rock right after your teacher finishes your lessons. Let's go swimming!"

Jacob started doing circles in the living room and hooting for joy. Amanda booked the room, and Jacob couldn't wait for the chance to swim. Amanda was interested in seeing how the hydro therapy would work for Jacob.

Tuesday was non-stop movement until they got to the hotel. They got Jackson to school, Ally to a babysitter, and then drove to physical therapy. They learned some exercises to try in the pool, and then rushed back to meet the teacher for the homebound program. For the second week in a row, she said she had other things to do and left early. It didn't bother Amanda and Jacob today since they had to jump in the car and drive to Little Rock.

Amanda pushed Jacob to the pool after dropping off their bags and changing into swimsuits. They looked at the chair lift for a few minutes, but Amanda decided to just get Jacob in the water without it. She put his chair next to the steps, then lifted him up and put him on the first step. Jacob held onto the handrail to help Amanda as she lowered him into the pool one step at a time.

Once in the water, Amanda was able to stand behind him and hold him up with ease. Jacob swung his arms back and forth repeatedly in a slow and steady motion. His left arm was able to keep up with his right surprisingly well in the water. Then Jacob kicked around a little. The lack of weight helped him to move his legs in a way he hadn't been able to do for five weeks. All his movements were slow and steady, but he was happy. Amanda moved around the pool, giving Jacob a feeling of motion as he did slow scissor kicks and alternating up and down kicks.

"How are you feeling Jacob?" Amanda asked a few times during the exercises.

"I feel free," Jacob said. "Everything feels lighter. I can move my arm and legs better than I can on that table in physical therapy. I don't feel as much pain either. I want to do this more often. I know it will help me get stronger faster."

"Well, then we will figure out a way to make this a regular part of your exercises," Amanda said. "We will just have to ask some friends since we can't come up to this hotel every day."

Chapter 33
Leg Work

When Amanda and Jacob got to their doctor's appointment, they were excited to let him know that they had just tried the hydro therapy the night before and how it helped with Jacob's pain and movement. The doctor was pleased to hear it and was also happy to let them know that Jacob's pelvic bone and vertebrae were healing really well.

"It has been just over six weeks since we fixed your pelvic bone, and it looks like it's almost completely healed," the doctor explained. "I think we should hold off on walking for just two more weeks, but take this note to your physical therapist. It explains that Jacob can start building muscle and putting weight on his lower extremities. Then in two weeks, barring any setbacks, we should be able to give you the green light to start standing and then walking."

"I thought we were told 4-6 weeks no pressure," Amanda said. "Has there been a problem that's delaying us two weeks, or is it just a precaution?"

"No, there hasn't been any problem," replied the doctor. "We are being a little extra cautious because of the abdominal trauma he experienced, and the fact we won't see you for two weeks. He could probably stand on the bones now, but he needs to build the muscle up to hold himself up first. So let's start there, and then he should be ready to try walking in two weeks."

Amanda and Jacob were pleased that the time to try walking was only two weeks away - barring any setbacks. That qualifying statement nagged at Amanda more than

Jacob. He was anxious to get back on his feet and only wished he was coming back to see the orthopedic doctor sooner so he could try walking next week.

The next day at the physical therapy session, they told Lon the good news. Lon had anticipated Jacob getting more freedom that week, so he was ready with some muscle strengthening exercises.

"Because you have worked so hard at the stretching and range of motion, I know you will work hard at the exercises I give you today," Lon said to Jacob. "You just have to promise me you will pay attention to the pain you feel. A little means we are working. A sharp pain means we are pushing too hard and need to stop."

Jacob agreed, and they started working. Jacob showed that he had worked on lifting his arm to 90 degrees or parallel with the ground, so Lon gave him a stretchy band to use as resistance. It was thin and didn't offer a lot of resistance, but Lon said he would give him a stronger one next week if he showed improvement. They had Jacob lay down, and Amanda took off his shoes. Jacob slid his feet side to side and then pulled them up close to his bottom before sliding them back down. These and a few other exercises were given to Jacob along with similar hydro therapy exercises to be done each day or as often as possible by their next appointment on Tuesday.

While Jacob was working with Lon, Amanda made a phone call to her friend that lived in Oak Grove, Louisiana, a neighboring community. Her friend had a pool and was happy to let Jacob and Amanda come use it anytime they wanted. Amanda arranged to start using her friend's pool that day, since it was only 11:00 am when they left the clinic. They got home, ate lunch and changed into their swimsuits.

Much like at the hotel pool, Amanda put the wheelchair close to the steps that led into the pool. She brought a patio chair and set it next to the wheelchair. Amanda slid Jacob onto the patio chair, and then lifted him onto the first step of the pool. They moved carefully down two steps. Finally, Amanda picked him up under the arms, and they began their exercises.

Jacob did everything Lon had asked him to do a couple times. Amanda pulled him along, reminding him of some of the suggested movements. She liked the pool therapy because Jacob was most comfortable in the water. She wished he could spend more time in the pool. But after about an hour, they worked back up the stairs and onto the patio chair where Jacob dried off. Amanda slid him back up on his wheelchair. Jacob tried to help as much as he could whenever he had something to grab onto. He often looked for opportunities like this to to use his arms more. He wanted to improve his arm strength and coordination.

On the way home, Amanda asked Jacob if he wanted to try going back to school for an hour or so. Jacob was excited and asked if he could take his electric wheelchair.

"No, I'm afraid you would run over someone," Amanda said. "Maybe some friends will help push you around for a while."

"Dang," Jacob said. "I was thinking it would be fun to zoom through the halls."

"That's precisely why it will stay at home," Amanda replied. "Plus we don't have a way of transporting it. We will just use it around the house."

After a pause, Amanda continued, "I will go talk to the principal when we get home. I think we will start out with just an hour at first, and see how you do."

"I think I can handle an hour of school," Jacob said.

Amanda pulled into the carport beside her house but didn't push Jacob inside. She walked him across the street and over to the principal's office. The principal was happy to see Jacob out and about and even helping to push his own wheels. When Amanda said they would like to try attending part of school a couple days the following week, the principal was surprised.

"So soon after getting out of the hospital," he said. "Are you ready Jacob?"

"Yes, sir," Jacob responded. "I think I can stay for an hour. I would like to try and see how it goes."

"The biggest problem will be his pain," Amanda said. "He

can't go to the bathroom on his own either, so that's why we will probably just try an hour a day next week. If it goes well, he may go longer, or if he isn't comfortable, he may skip a day. We will just have to see how it goes. Will that work?"

"I think that should be okay," the principal said. "My only concern is that it may be a disruption to the class to have him coming and going. I think we can minimize that effect if Jacob is here at the beginning of the day and sits in the back. Then he can quietly excuse himself or contact you to come get him."

They agreed on that plan. Then Amanda pushed Jacob back home so he could rest.

Chapter 34
Back to School

When Jacob woke up on Friday morning, he felt sore. It wasn't just his legs either. He felt sharp pains inside his lower chest, and he was doubled over crying from the pain. Amanda was worried and wasn't sure if she should call 911 or if she should just have him rest. She called the Little Rock Hospital nurse that worked with patients after they went home. Amanda explained to her what Jacob was feeling and when it started. She told the nurse everything she could think of, whether it seemed important or not.

When Amanda was finished, the nurse explained, "As scary as this looks to you, I think we are dealing with scar tissue in his diaphragm. He doesn't have a fever, and he isn't having bloody stool. If he starts exhibiting any of those signs, immediately go to the hospital. It is common to have scar tissue develop on internal lacerations that are repaired. While painful, we can't really do anything for it. The body will take care of it in time. What Jacob needs to do is lay down, take some pain medicine and try to relax."

"Should we scale back his physical therapy?" Amanda asked. She was worried the exercise had caused the sudden pain.

"For now, he should just rest, but once the pain goes away, you can do low-stress exercises," the nurse said. "It's probably not the exercise that started this pain. His diaphragm constantly moves when he breathes, and exercises can make him breath deeper and harder, but he has to get through it so he can walk again. If he has a physical therapy appointment today, you might need to cancel it just so Jacob can rest. Otherwise, he should be through the worst of it within the next 24 to 48 hours."

Two days of watching Jacob hurting like this was not comforting news to Amanda or Jacob. She gave him some Ibuprofen and let him lay on the couch. He cycled between crying and moaning to a fitful sleep for most of the day. Amanda tried everything she could think of to help him get comfortable, but it didn't seem to help much. She almost called the school and said she would wait another week, but decided to wait it out. She could make that decision Monday morning if she needed to.

Saturday was much better. Jacob woke up without any sharp pains - only a little soreness but it was managable - and he really wanted to go swimming. Amanda took Jacob, Jackson, and Ally to her friend's pool. Her friend was happy to see the whole crew and helped keep an eye on Ally in the water. Amanda went through the tedious process of getting Jacob into the water, but once he was there, Jacob was happy and moved around like he had before. He tried not to push himself too hard so he wouldn't trigger more abdominal cramps.

Jackson and Ally watched Jacob more than they swam. They were curious about how he would get therapy in the water. Jackson would always watch at home when Amanda stretched and moved Jacob for his daily exercises and was ready to help if she asked for anything. In the shallow end, Ally would play a little, then watch Jacob, play for a while longer and then watch Jacob again.

After Jacob had gone through all his exercises, he sat on the lowest step while Amanda played with Ally for 10 minutes. Jackson went over to Jacob and made up a little game for them to play squirting water through their hands. When it was time to go, Amanda made her way up the stairs with Jacob and then onto the patio chair just as she had done on Thursday. Jacob dried off, and then Amanda moved him into his wheelchair.

Jacob was a little sore the next day, but nothing like he

had been Friday morning. They all got up in time to go to church. Amanda thought that if they would give school a chance on Monday, they should give God a chance on Sunday.

Everyone at church was happy to see Amanda and Jacob. They caused such a stir that the meeting was delayed 10 minutes from its normal starting time. Jacob did well through the first 30 minutes of church but found he got more and more uncomfortable as the sermon continued. He was happy when they started playing music because it gave him a chance to ask Amanda to shift him without disturbing anyone. They made it through the full hour of church services, and Jacob was pleased he could sit that long. It gave him confidence for going to school. Amanda and her kids were all happy they had gone to church. The good feeling they felt during the sermon continued throughout the rest of the day.

Monday morning was a rush to get everyone ready in time. Amanda had everyone ready before school just about every day the last three weeks, but she felt a little more anxiety this morning which made her feel rushed. Jacob said he felt like normal: achy but manageable. Amanda gave him some Tylenol, and they went to school. Jackson pushed Jacob the whole way and offered to take Jacob to his class. Amanda refused his help so she could make sure the teacher understood Jacob's needs and how they planned to proceed.

All of Jacob's friends - and even others that didn't know him that well - said hello to him and said they were glad to see him. Jacob was kind of embarrassed about the sudden popularity. Thankfully, the first bell rang shortly after they arrived and the crowd students went to their classes.

The bell also helped to end the awkward conversations. Everyone wanted to know about the tractor incident. Amanda thought that would be the case, so after a couple kids asked and Jacob didn't respond, she told everyone that the experience was hard to talk about right now. Maybe Jacob would be able to share more about it later, but she asked them to please try not to ask about it for a while.

Amanda wheeled Jacob into his classroom and saw that a table was set for him in the back of the room. The teacher came up and welcomed Jacob into the class.

"It's good to have you with us, Jacob," Ms. Jones said. "You have been doing well with your school work we've been sending home. If you have any questions, please let me know, and I will answer them as best I can."

"I'm not sure if the principal explained our plan, but due to Jacob's injuries, we aren't sure how long he will be able to sit in class," Amanda explained. "Jacob is going to stay as long as he can, but he gets painfully uncomfortable after sitting in one position for very long. When he needs to come home, he will text me, and I will come get him. We don't want to disturb the class if we can help it, so if you or another child can help Jacob out of the room, he can wheel himself down to the office, and I will come get him. The hope is that as Jacob gets stronger and heals more, he will be able to stay in class longer and longer."

Ms. Jones agreed that she was happy to comply with this plan and just asked Jacob to let her know when he needed to be excused. She would have Sabrina, his classmate that sat next to him, open the door for him.

Jacob sat through the first 30 minutes of the day without too many problems. Sabrina helped show Jacob where they were and helped him get his books out on the table. Ms. Jones started the day with math. When she asked all the students to work on the problems on page 32, Jacob felt the common ache beginning to get stronger. He tried to reposition himself in his wheelchair, and it helped for a few minutes, but he only got through half of his assignment before shifting in his seat wouldn't ease the pain. He waited as long as he could, but just as they were moving on to another subject, Jacob texted his mom and let Ms. Jones know he needed to leave. Sabrina helped open the door for Jacob and offered to push him down to the office.

Amanda got to the office just moments after Jacob and pushed him home so he could lay down and get some relief from his back pain.

"Well, at least you were able to go for an hour," Amanda said, as they walked toward the house. "That's pretty good for your first day. Hopefully, as we continue to go through the physical therapy, your body will be able to sit longer. Maybe we need to have you sit in this chair longer during the day so you can learn to get comfortable in it."

"Maybe," Jacob said. "I still think you should let me take the electric wheelchair to school."

"No chance," Amanda said. They chuckled together as they entered the house.

Jacob went to his bed to rest, but he used his straps to do a few exercises before laying down to relax. He wasn't that tired, but laying down helped to relieve the pain for a while.

Chapter 35
Shuffle

The next day, Jacob didn't go to school at all because he had physical therapy in the morning and the homebound teacher was coming in the afternoon. Therapy went well, and Jacob showed he was able to pull his legs up to his bottom and slide them out to the side with little problem. Jacob liked getting exercises he could do on his own so he could work on them when Amanda was busy.

Lon helped Jacob sit up in a chair and then put small 2.5-pound weights on Jacob's ankles. He asked Jacob to slide his feet out in front of him and then back in. Jacob's sock covered feet, moved slowly over the tile floor.

"You can do this at home anywhere there is a tile or flat, smooth surface," Lon said to Jacob. "Do this five times back and forth, then put your feet half way out and move them side to side five times. Let yourself rest in between, so you don't overdo it."

"Yes, sir," Jacob replied. He planned to sit in a chair in the kitchen while Amanda made dinner. "It's pretty easy, even with the weights. I think it's because we have gone to the pool a few times since our last visit."

"I can tell that you are making good progress," Lon said. "I also think it's because you are young and working hard at your exercises at home. I can tell the difference between the people who do their homework and the ones that only try to work at their appointments."

"I want to get walking again so I will do whatever you ask me to do at home," Jacob said enthusiastically as he slid his feet side to side.

After a couple other exercises for Jacob's lower body and core muscles, Lon focused on Jacob's left arm. Lon gave Jacob a stretchy band and asked him to pull it apart. As before, this band was light and didn't offer much resistance. Jacob pulled it apart and told Lon about the straps above his bed that he used to pull up on, though he wasn't able to pull himself all the way up yet. Lon applauded the effort, but reminded Jacob not to overdo it. He must always listen to his body about when to stop.

Amanda was proud of Jacob, and the work he was putting in. She couldn't have predicted how quickly he would recover, or how much time Jacob would put into his recovery. Amanda also knew he didn't do it alone. He had been blessed in his healing. She offered a silent prayer of gratitude for the speed of Jacob's recovery.

They made it home in time for Jacob to work with Ms. White. She stayed until 4:00 pm this time, and they were able to get through all of his school work. Amanda worked with Jackson on his homework for part of that time. At dinner, Jacob asked if they could go swimming again. Amanda said it wouldn't work out that night, but they would go after school the next day.

Jacob didn't sleep well that night. At school the next day, Jacob was in a depressed mood. He was annoyed at how much others had to do for him. His depression deepened when he noticed Amanda holding her back after loading him in the car. Seeing Jackson run over to his friends when they got to school only reminded Jacob how limited he was in a wheelchair. Kids wanted to push him down the hall, but the attention bothered him because it reminded him he was crippled right now. On top of all that, Jacob's body was sore from the incident, operations, and therapy.

He stayed at school for an hour and a half. He might have stayed longer, but nature called, and it was a good excuse to leave. When he asked to be let out, Sabrina wanted to push him back down the hall. Jacob curtly declared he wanted to roll himself this time.

Amanda brought him home and as she cleaned him up, Jacob asked, "When will I be normal again?"

Amanda was a little surprised by the question.

"You have been making great progress," Amanda said. "You are making huge strides at physical therapy. You are controlling your bladder more and more each week. You had a rough night last night, but it seems like you are sleeping better lately."

Jacob was quiet.

"We don't know when you will be back to normal," Amanda said, deciding it's better to level with Jacob rather than try to pretend life was all roses. "When we were in the hospital, I was worried we would be looking at years in a wheelchair. But with the progress you've made since we've been home from the hospital, I think you will be back to normal much sooner than anyone could have guessed."

"I don't like being this way," Jacob said in a quiet voice. "I just want to play with my brother and friends again. I want to get up and go when I want to, and on my own two feet."

"You will Jacob," Amanda said, putting her hand on his head. "God has blessed you to get this far. Trust in Him and He will get you back to normal soon enough.

"I also think some rest will help you feel better," Amanda suggested. "Do you want to lay down for a nap?"

Jacob agreed and fell asleep thinking about what his mother said. He slept for an hour and felt much better. He asked to get in a chair in the kitchen so he could do his exercises. When Amanda moved the wheelchair into position, he used his straps to pull himself up to a sitting position. Amanda helped a little in the middle. Then he used his arms to help move onto the wheelchair. Amanda appreciated his desire to lift with her. It showed he was not giving up.

Once Jackson got home, Amanda took all the kids to the pool. Jacob was able to move a little faster than before through his exercises. Jackson played with Ally until Jacob was finished with his therapy. As Amanda took some time to play with Ally, she looked back at the steps where the boys were laughing with each other. For an instant, it seemed almost like life was back to normal - like so many other times when they had gone swimming or playing at a lake. She felt the familiar feeling that she had experienced before. This was what she was supposed to be doing and where she needed to be now. She had her kids and they were happy. Life was good.

The following day at the clinic, Jacob was graduated to five-pound weights on each foot. He went through all of his exercises, struggling a little at times, but pushing through each task. Lon told Jacob that he thought they could try standing and taking a couple steps if Jacob wanted to. Jacob's eyes opened wide. He didn't think the day would ever come; now it was here. He bobbed his head enthusiastically.

"You think he's ready?" Amanda asked, thinking this was really quick.

"I do," Lon said. "You told me the doctor was ready to release him nearly two weeks ago but wanted to wait a little longer to be cautious. The progress Jacob has made already tells me he is ready to at least stand up, with help. We will try it today and see how it goes. If it hurts, we will know he isn't ready. It's already been more than seven weeks since his surgery. The bones should be healed enough to let him stand."

Amanda didn't have any arguments with that line of thinking. She watched as Lon stood behind the chair Jacob was standing in and helped to lift Jacob onto his feet. Jacob was shaky, but he didn't have any sharp pains. It was like he was trying to stand still during an earthquake.

Amanda saw the huge grin on Jacob's face. He was so excited to be able to stand again. Amanda started to cry.

Jacob sat down, and Lon asked about the pain.

"No sir," Jacob said. "It didn't hurt at all. It felt really good. Can we take a couple steps?"

"We can try that," Lon said. "I will be right behind you."

So again, Lon helped Jacob stand up, and Jacob cautiously and slowly moved his right foot forward three inches. Then he pulled his left foot forward and placed it down three inches in front of the right one. He took six steps and then Amanda put the chair behind him and Lon helped him sit down. Now Jacob was the one with tears in his eyes.

Chapter 36
Shooting At Fish

Jacob was able to go to school for 2.5 hours that Friday. Many of his friends were happy to push his wheelchair and hold his books. During a break in class, he told Sabrina that he finally took some steps at physical therapy. She was happy for him and asked what other things he did at therapy. He explained a few of the exercises he did, but then class got started again. Half way through English, Jacob needed to go to the bathroom. He texted his mom and she came to get him. Jacob wanted to go back, so after he got cleaned up, he went back for lunch with his friends and half an hour more of class. Then his pain was too much to bear, so he went home for the rest of the day.

Amanda decided that with Jacob starting to go to school more frequently, she could probably start taking on part-time work. Now she had to decide what to do about where she would work. Would she try to get her old job back, or should she look for another job? She had missed the test to become an insurance agent since she was at the hospital in Little Rock. They would probably not be willing to spend another $300 for her to take it again. She really needed a job and her options were limited, but would the insurance agency even be willing to bring her back on with the understanding that she wouldn't be full time right away and at any moment she could be called away? It would be a hard discussion to have, but she needed to face it.

That morning after Jacob went to school the first time, Amanda called Granny to see if she could come and sit with

Jacob that afternoon. She said that was fine, so once Jacob was home and situated, she called Granny again and she came to sit with Jacob.

Amanda got in the car and headed back to her old office building. When she pulled up she had flashbacks of the day she left in a rush to see Jacob at the hospital across the Arkansas border. Pushing those thoughts out of her head, Amanda walked up to the door. As she walked in, she saw that someone else was sitting at her old desk. She saw that some of her pictures were still sitting on the desk and she knew she had some personal things in the draws.

"Amanda, what an unexpected surprise," said her former boss. Amanda could tell it was as awkward for him as it was for her to see that they had already moved on. She was seeing that the conversation she dreaded wasn't going to happen.

"Yeah, I just wanted to come by and get my things," Amanda said, not wanting to prolong the moment any more than necessary.

"Did you want to talk about continuing to work for us?" he asked, forcing a smile. "We could probably work something out."

"No, I just need a box if you have one," Amanda said. She actually was feeling a little relieved already. They gave her a box and asked how Jacob was doing. Amanda gave polite answers but focused on getting her things packed up and then left.

When she walked out, she realized two things immediately. She felt peace about her decision. She was relieved to have that over with. The second thing that occurred to her was that she didn't have a clue what she would do. She would spend some time that weekend thinking and praying about what she should do for work. She wouldn't try to start working until Jacob was back at school full time and could use the bathroom on his own. She had some time, so she wouldn't stress about it, but she would start looking around soon.

Amanda thought to herself, *It's strange that I feel so relieved after walking away from the only job prospect I had at a time when I need money more than ever, but I feel peace.*

That evening Jackson and Ally went to their dad's house for the weekend. Jacob watched some TV that night, but after breakfast Saturday morning he was bored. Amanda had things she needed to take care of so she couldn't entertain Jacob. Jacob decided to go outside.

After driving his electric wheelchair around the driveway five or six times, he didn't see anything that peaked his interest. He was almost ready to go in and lay on the couch when he decided to go look at the pond.

Next to the house and beside the driveway was a 40-gallon pond with half a dozen fish in it. They lazily swam around in the water, heedless of Jacob watching them.

I bet I could shoot one of them, Jacob thought. Without further consideration, he zoomed inside and grabbed his little bow and arrow set. He didn't say anything to Amanda about his plan, and she was busy with something else. She didn't see the bow in his lap as he drove back outside.

Jacob knocked an arrow and took aim at the fattest fish. He pulled back as far as he could and when he thought he had his shot, he let the arrow fly.

He didn't hit a fish.

He did puncture the pond liner.

As the water started to drain, Jacob began yelling for his mom.

"What's wrong Jacob," Amanda cried as she came running out the side door.

Embarrassed at his silly mistake, he didn't say anything for a minute.

Amanda was confused and upset at first, once she saw that the water level was dropping in the pond.

What was he thinking? Amanda asked herself. She didn't want to yell, and she could see that the water was draining, so she ran in for a large pot and put the fish in the pot with some water. She turned to look at Jacob.

"Are you going to cook 'em?" Jacob asked, hoping the joke would help to lighten the mood.

Amanda sighed at first and then started to laugh.

"That was pretty dumb, I admit," Jacob said, laughing a little too. "I can't believe I missed."

"Why were you going to shoot it in the first place?" Amanda asked, with a pleading tone. She couldn't understand how the thought even crossed his mind.

"I don't know," Jacob said. "Just bored, I guess."

Amanda had to have pity on her son. He was bored and highly limited in his options for fun.

"Well, I don't want to keep those fish in that pot for long, so let's go to the store and get another liner," Amanda suggested and started heading inside. When they got to the hardware store, they didn't have the size of liner Amanda needed. She had to get a bigger one.

So for the rest of the day, Amanda dug a larger hole in the ground to accommodate the new lining. Jacob felt bad because he wasn't able to help. He stayed outside with Amanda for moral support. There were a few times when Amanda stopped to give her sore back a break. She would look at Jacob and start laughing to herself.

Chapter 37
Ring Around the Table

At physical therapy on September 7, Jacob once again was able to stand and shuffle his feet a few times and then sit back down. After doing a few more exercises, Lon put the 2.5-pound weights on Jacob's feet and had him try walking again. It was obviously harder on Jacob, but he managed to walk three feet before sitting down. Jacob had continued to work on his flexibility and prescribed exercises at home every day. Amanda was able to take Jacob to the pool a few more times as well, and Jacob was getting stronger with his kicks.

"You are making some incredible progress, Jacob," Lon said. "You are working hard at home, I can tell. How are you feeling?"

"I'm feeling some pain nearly all the time," Jacob said with a shrug. "The exercises don't really make it worse. At first, I was sore, but I don't feel that sore anymore."

"You aren't having any more intense pains in your abdomen like you did a couple weeks ago?" Lon asked, glancing at Amanda.

"No, he hasn't," Amanda answered. "He is sleeping a little better at night and can sit in school a little longer too, so I think the therapy is helping his pain, not adding to it."

Jacob was thrilled that he was starting to walk more. He would have tried to walk 10 feet if Lon had let him. He wanted to run. He decided he would find a way to practice walking at home.

Jacob met with Ms. White shortly after Amanda and Jacob

got home from physical therapy. They reviewed his work and practiced some of the new math assignments he had been given as homework. After Ms. White left, Amanda started to work on dinner. Jacob parked his electronic wheelchair next to the kitchen table. When his Mom left the room, he decided to get up and try walking. He leaned on the table and made his way down the long side. Then worried he wouldn't have the strength to go all the way around, he went back to his seat. He was just getting to his chair when his mom walked back into the room.

"What are you doing?" Amanda asked as she rushed over to help him get back in his seat. She was surprised to see him up, but not surprised he was trying to walk now that he had done it twice at the clinic.

"I'm just practicing," Jacob said. He was breathing heavily from the exertion.

"Just because the therapist lets you take a couple steps doesn't mean you can start walking around on your own," Amanda said. "You don't want to fall, do you? I will help support you if you want to try walking, but please don't do it on your own."

"Yes, Ma'am," Jacob said. "It feels so good to be able to walk again. Can we try walking in the pool?"

"I suppose, but we won't be going to the pool today or tomorrow," Amanda replied. "We have another appointment in Little Rock tomorrow."

"Again?" Jacob asked in dismay. "When are we going to be done making that long trip?"

"We have two more, I think," Amanda answered and then walked to the calendar. "After tomorrow, we will have made four trips. I think they said we would have five follow-up visits. So tomorrow and then one more, I believe."

Amanda and Jacob were off to Little Rock as soon as Jackson went to school and Ally was at the babysitters. On the way, they talked about how school was going. Jacob said he thought he could make it through four hours of school now. He just needed Amanda to come get him for one bathroom break in the middle of those four hours. Amanda

pointed out that with Jacob walking a little they may move
him to crutches, and he may be able to go to the bathroom
by himself soon. Jacob felt like he got his independence
back with those words, though he knew he needed to work
on his arm strength to use crutches. It was something to
work toward, not an immediate result just because it was
suggested.

The doctor had a little different idea though.

"It's wonderful that you are beginning to walk," the
physician said. "The fact that you are walking this soon after
surgery is a true result of your hard work. Many would take
it slower, especially if it meant missing more school."

Jacob smiled at the compliment.

"I don't think crutches will be good for you," the doctor
continued. "They would put an undue amount of stress on
your left armpit and may slow down your progress. I think
it would be better to use a walker until you are ready to
walk on your own."

Jacob was mortified at the suggestion of a walker.
He immediately imagined he would have gray hair and
wrinkles if he used a walker. He wanted to protest, but
Amanda was nodding her head in approval of the plan.
There wasn't anything else for him to do, but go along with
it. It would be more motivation to get to walking on his own
faster.

Amanda saw in Jacob's face that he didn't like the idea
of using a walker. She understood the reasons for using a
walker though, so she knew they would just have to work it
out. *He didn't like the urine bottle, but he got used to it,* Amanda
thought. *Besides, it wouldn't be too long before he is walking
normally again; he is progressing so quickly.*

The doctor cleared Jacob to do full exercises and start
strengthening exercises as much as he was able. They should
still follow the physical therapist's suggestions, but there
was no reason to avoid any exercises the therapist saw fit
to try. There was one last appointment in two weeks, and
then Jacob would have six months before he needed another
check up.

Amanda and Jacob were excited about that news. As they were getting ready to leave, Amanda thought the walker would be the only problem they would have to work on, but as they were headed toward the exit of the doctor's office, the receptionist called her back. Amanda thought it was so she could schedule the last appointment.

"Ms. Brown, we've been talking to your insurance provider, and they said they won't be covering these follow-up visits since it's out of network and not an emergency," the receptionist said. "I'm afraid we will have to send you the bill. Would you like to schedule your final visit with us, or go to another doctor?"

Amanda was blindsided by this information. What would they do? Starting a new doctor for one visit seemed silly and what was another doctor's visit on top of $75,000? They would make their last appointment and then schedule an in-state orthopedic doctor for any further checkups Jacob needed after that. Amanda made the appointment, and they left.

In the car, Jacob and Amanda were lost in their own thoughts for 45 minutes. Jacob wondered how long everyone would laugh at him for using a walker. Would he have the ridiculous tennis balls on the back legs too? Why not just use crutches?

Amanda's thoughts were centered on how to keep her family afloat. She needed Jacob to go back to school so she could start working, but she couldn't just throw him out on his own. Who would clean him up and help him when the pain flared up? What would she do when he was able to go to school all day long? How much would the five follow-up visits add to her already out-of-control debt from this one incident? She hoped her lawyer was able to get the farm insurance company to help pay the bills.

It was Jacob that spoke first - breaking their separate trains of thought.

"Mom, I really don't want to have a walker," Jacob said, crossing his arms.

"I know it's not cool, but you heard the doctor," Amanda

reasoned. "He said it's better than crutches. I agree with him. Besides, they gave me an order form and helped to order one already. We should have your walker by Friday."

"Really," Jacob said, his voice between panic and dejection. "Old people use walkers."

"Oh, come on," Amanda said, not able to hide the smile on her face. "Other people use walkers too. Anybody that needs help walking for a while can use a walker. Crutches aren't really much cooler."

It was quiet for another 10 minutes. Amanda was racking her brain trying to find a way to make a walker look cool. She couldn't add a lot of weight to it. She didn't want to spend a ton of money either because he may only be in it for a few weeks. He had to use it though to keep getting stronger at walking, so they needed to do something with it.

"What if we make it look cool?" Amanda said, still not sure how she would pull it off.

Jacob looked incredulous; as if to say, 'by what miracle would you make a walker look cool?'

"Well, maybe it won't be cool, but it won't look like anyone else's walker," Amanda said. "It will be fine."

Chapter 38
Walker

The next day at physical therapy, Amanda told Lon about their doctor prescribing a walker for Jacob. He didn't seem phased by the recommendation of walker over crutches. He found a walker they would practice with there since Jacob hadn't received his yet. Jacob looked at the aluminum walker and privately groaned. But Jacob knew Lon and his mom wouldn't make fun of him, so he participated with his usual vigor and soon he was walking 20 steps across the room. It made him tired, but it was exhilarating. Lon showed him a variety of leg and core exercises that would help him get stronger, aside from just walking.

Next, they worked on Jacob's arms. Lon gave Jacob a stretchy band that supplied a lot more tension than before. Lon told Jacob to stretch the band by pulling his arms out to the sides. Jacob's face was full of concentration and his upper lip curled as he struggled to make his left arm match his right arm.

Lon gave him the band and told him to do that exercise and a few more to continue to strengthen his arm at home. The walker would help strengthen his arm too, but Lon wanted to work out a variety of muscles so Jacob could get full use from his arm. Lon also performed some massages to help break up the scar tissue underneath the skin.

Jacob had already started using his left hand for a variety of activities, such as eating, pulling himself out of bed and rolling his wheelchair. These activities were usually slow and awkward, but Jacob didn't mind. He wanted to challenge himself so he could get better control over his arm.

After physical therapy, Amanda took Jacob back home and he met with Ms. White. Her visit was shortened again, so Amanda took Jacob to the pool for some more exercises. Jacob asked that they practice walking in the pool, too. At first, Amanda was apprehensive, but she agreed and held Jacob's sides as he walked back and forth across the three-foot deep section of the pool. It felt easier to walk in the pool, though he did have water resistance against his legs. Jacob had to learn to keep his balance again, which was a struggle at first.

Jacob went to school for a couple hours on Friday. When Amanda brought him home to give him a bathroom break around 10:00 am, Jacob's walker arrived. It was shiny and aluminum. Jacob still didn't like it. Amanda said she had an idea and she would go to the store for a couple things while Jacob went back to school.

Jacob was distracted the next hour and a half at school, wondering what his mom was going to do to the walker. He hoped she would put antlers on it or hang alligator teeth on it. He just didn't want it to be plain, silver, and look like all the other old-man walkers he had seen. When he couldn't handle the discomfort any longer, he texted Amanda to let her know he was done. She had a slight smile on her face when she walked in to get him. When he asked her why she was smiling, she just said, "You'll see."

After they walked into the house, Amanda went to her room and brought out the walker. Jacob was surprised by what he saw. The walker was covered in camouflage duct tape. Not only did it not look old, it also reminded him about one of the reasons he wanted to get back on his feet again. He couldn't wait to go camping and hunting again. It was simple, but it made Jacob feel better about eventually taking a walker to school. Jacob used it to walk across the house, and then he rested. He walked into the bathroom and used the toilet for the first time in more than a month. It was like getting his freedom back. He still couldn't control his bladder all the time, but this was definitely progress.

When Jackson got home, he was a little envious of Jacob's walker. He wanted a camouflage walking stick to match his brother's walker. Jackson was proud of his brother's hard work and recovery so far. Jackson walked right behind Jacob as he took another lap around the front room - content to walk at Jacob's pace.

Jackson didn't know how to put it in words to Amanda and Jacob, but that night as he read in the Bible and said his prayers he thought about how amazing it was that Jacob was walking again. He thought back to seeing his brother, bleeding and groaning on the back seat of the truck. He thought back to the first time he saw Jacob in a coma in the hospital. Jackson remembered getting to talk to Jacob once he woke up from the coma. Jackson had worried Jacob would never walk again and even still wondered if Jacob would live. His mom told him Jacob would be fine, but she frequently had tears in her eyes.

Jackson had a tear in his eye now. He didn't know how, but he knew God had made Jacob better again. Jackson read about the miracles Jesus did, and Jackson knew Jesus had healed his brother. Jackson remembered the therapy and exercises that Jacob did all the time so he could get better. Jacob had done his part, and the Lord was making him whole. Jackson offered a prayer that night, full of gratitude for the miracle he was witnessing.

Jacob too was happy and full of gratitude. He was farther along in his recovery than he had ever dared to hope. He knew it wasn't just his hard work either. He had given his best effort at doing exercises at home each day. He pushed himself each day, but he just knew it wasn't only him. He couldn't make his body whole again, but God was making it happen. He felt joy in overcoming an obstacle with God. It was something he hadn't felt before.

Amanda still had a lot of concerns on her mind, but she was reflecting on the way Jackson and Jacob walked around together. She loved that they were still close and supporting each other. Amanda looked at the calendar and realized that it was just two months before that Jacob had been run over. She thought about Jacob asking when he would walk, and how she didn't want to promise any time before Thanksgiving. Here they were in mid-September, and Jacob was walking with a walker. Like her sons, Amanda knew it wasn't just Jacob's effort that was speeding up his recovery. She knew God was making it possible. She thought about all the prayers that had been offered in their behalf and how many people had been personal angels when they needed it most. God had helped them come farther than they could have done alone so she would trust and be grateful for what He had done for them.

Chapter 39
Bullies

It was Monday, September 13, when Jacob tried to go to school most of the day, and they stopped the homebound program. Amanda knew it would still not be like a normal school day since Jacob needed help going to the bathroom, and the pain continued to bother him at times. Jacob wanted to try to go to as much school as he possible and just come home to take medicine or bathroom breaks as needed.

Monday was good, but there were frequent trips home. Tuesday, he went to physical therapy towards the end of the day, so he missed some classes. One of the classes was his history class, and he didn't turn in a paper that was due. He thought it wouldn't be a problem and he would turn it in on Wednesday.

Amanda went to pick up Jacob and Jackson after school on Wednesday, and Amanda saw that Jacob was crying. She asked him why, assuming it was probably pain related. Jacob just said he had a bad day, and it was nothing. Amanda didn't really believe that, but she didn't want to badger him.

They went home and worked on homework, but Jacob was sad and aloof. Amanda was concerned about him. She would give him a little time to work it out, but she would ask more questions the next day when they were headed to physical therapy. Jacob did perk up a little when Amanda encouraged him to practice walking and doing his exercises. She assumed it gave him something to think about and get his mind off the pain - or whatever was bothering him.

Jacob was not his usual self Thursday morning, and Amanda asked him if he felt OK. He said he did and he was excited to go to physical therapy. Amanda picked up Jacob from school to go to therapy, and Jacob was sad again. She got him loaded up and they headed toward Monroe, LA.

"Jacob, what's bothering you?" Amanda asked after a few minutes of silence.

Jacob just kept looking out the window. Then he said, "I don't want to talk about it yet."

The tense silence made the rest of the hour-long trip feel much longer. Amanda knew there was something wrong, and yet Jacob didn't want to talk about it. Were there kids making fun of him? Did they hurt him?

When they were 10 miles away from Monroe, Jacob said, "Yesterday, when I was in the office waiting for you around 1:30 pm. My history teacher came to the office. He looked at me and asked why I hadn't turned in my report on time. I said I had to go to physical therapy, and then he said, 'I thought they were working your legs, not picking your brain. Can't you finish your work on time?' I told him it was done, I just didn't get it turned in. He said, it better not happen again. I told him I'd miss his class again Thursday because of therapy. He said, 'It is just as well since you cry and complain so much when you are in my class.' And then he snickered and walked away."

"Jacob, why didn't you say something sooner?" Amanda said in an exasperated tone. "We could have got this straightened out yesterday or today."

"That's why I waited," Jacob said, still looking out the window. "I knew you would be mad, so I didn't want you to make a scene."

"But Jacob, you don't need to endure that kind of treatment from anyone, especially a teacher," Amanda said. "I will set up a parent-teacher meeting with the principal tomorrow."

While Jacob got started with his physical therapy, Amanda called the school. She set up a meeting with the principal, Jacob's history teacher and scheduled it during the teacher's open hour. Amanda was still trying to calm down when she joined Jacob and Lon in the therapy area. She focused on learning the new exercises Jacob should do. She didn't say anything else to Jacob about the teacher or what she would say to him. Amanda only said she had an appointment before his class the next day.

When Amanda sat down with the teacher and principal, Amanda could see some defiance veiled with civility in the teacher. The principal started the meeting off by saying that Ms. Brown had some concerns she wanted to discuss.

"My son came home rather upset after talking to you, and I just wanted to clarify the situation so it won't happen again," Amanda said looking directly at the history teacher. "He said that you asked if they were picking at his brain at physical therapy and that's why he didn't get his work turned in. You complained that he cried and whined about his pain in class. Is that true?"

"I may have said something along those lines, but I didn't mean to upset him," the history teacher said, surprised at how quickly it was coming out. "I have Rheumatoid Arthritis. My hands and wrists leave me in constant pain, but my condition affects my breathing too. I try not to complain about it, though. He complains in class, and it's distracting to the students."

"Do you have any idea what he has been through?" Amanda said, fighting to keep her emotions in check. "It was only two months ago that Jacob had a 15-ton tractor roll across his abdomen and break his pelvic bone. He had nearly all his internal organs displaced and the blood pressure was so high, he couldn't even see me when I got to him at the hospital. It took more than four hours in two surgeries to get his organs back in place and his pelvic bone fixed with a twelve-inch plate. His arm was nearly cut off, his back was fractured, and he was in a coma for a week."

The principal and teacher were silent, eyes wide as they heard the gruesome details.

"He has battled back from all those injuries and is finally starting to walk," Amanda said, tears starting to come to her eyes. "All those injuries don't just heal without pain. He has been dealing with multiple fractures and internal scar tissue that is extremely painful. He doesn't have anything stronger than Ibuprofen and Tylenol to manage his pain. Anything stronger makes him drowsy. So he has to fight through the pain, but he wants to come to school. I'm not pushing him, he wants to be here."

"I didn't know ..." the history teacher began but was cut off by Amanda.

"You don't understand what we are dealing with," Amanda said. "I sleep with a baby monitor next to my bed so I can move him multiple times during the night. Even six weeks after coming home from the hospital, I have to get up with him at least three times a night. It used to be every 45 minutes when we first got home. He doesn't get normal sleep. Did you realize he has to wear a diaper because no one can help him use the toilet here? He's trying to get his confidence back. He's trying to just be normal again, but these are real issues he has to deal with. Is he asking everyone for pity? No! He just wants to get back to school with his friends."

"I didn't realize he was struggling with these things," the history teacher said.

"I don't fully understand everything you are dealing with," Amanda said, her voice softer but still charged. "I don't need to understand everything to know I should be a decent human being toward you. He should be safe at school, especially with teachers. Please stop picking on my child."

"I am so sorry," the teacher began again. "I didn't mean to hurt his feelings."

"What I want to know is this," Amanda said, turning her attention back to the principal. "Should we take him out of school, and continue the homebound program until Jacob is completely healthy, which may be a while longer, or can he keep trying to get back into regular school like he wants to?"

"I think we can do what's best for Jacob," the principal said. His face showed that he was disturbed by the situation, and he truly felt bad for what happened. "If Jacob wants to keep coming to school, that would be fine with us." He meant all the school staff in his collective 'us,' but motioned toward the history teacher since he was sitting in the room. He nodded his head silently.

"One more thing," Amanda said to the principal as she stood to leave. "Jackson saw the whole thing. He saw his brother get pulled from the dirt. He held his brother on the back seat of a pickup as Jacob bled from his nose and ears and mouth. He saw his brother get life flighted to the children's hospital and still has nightmares about that horrible day. I'm not asking you to treat him differently from any other child, but he's healing too."

Amanda looked at the history teacher as she concluded that thought, "You don't know what these kids are going through, so don't pick on them."

There wasn't much said as Amanda walked out of the principal's office. Amanda went home and to relax on the couch for a while to let her heart beat slow down, and her blood pressure return to normal. She recognized that the teacher was dealing with his own pain, and had to keep going with his job. That wasn't any reason to talk down to the children. Were there other kids treated the same way? Amanda had no idea. It just seemed like she shouldn't have to struggle so much to get Jacob back into school.

Amanda went back to the school to help Jacob use the restroom and get some pain medicine. It was before he went to his history class, so they didn't talk about the parent-teacher meeting. After school, Amanda picked up Jacob and Jackson as usual. As Amanda was helping Jacob get into the car, Jacob said, "I don't know what you said, but it sure did help. He didn't say anything mean to me. He even tried to be nice to me."

"Good," Amanda said, not smiling about the victory. "You didn't deserve to be treated that way in the first place. Hopefully, it won't happen again."

Chapter 40
Walk In School

Jackson and Ally were gone to their dad's house that weekend, so Jacob practiced walking the length of the house. By Sunday night, he was able to walk down and back without a break. It made him tired, but he was bursting with joy to walk again.

Jacob told his friends that he was starting to walk again. Jacob still had to come home for bathroom breaks, but he was starting to go much longer without soiling his diaper. He was beginning to feel confident about controlling his bowels again. In fact, when he went home for those breaks, he used his walker to go to the bathroom on his own. It was really liberating for the 10-year-old.

At physical therapy on September 21, Jacob started off with by showing Lon how well he was getting around on a walker. Lon watched with evident surprise on his face.

"That's incredible," Lon said. "In the 10 years I have been doing physical therapy, I have never seen someone get run over and then get back to walking so quickly. You have progressed through the exercises faster than anyone would have predicted. It's a testament to your hard work and young body."

"I think it's a testament to God's power to work miracles," Amanda said. Jacob smiled and nodded back. "Jacob is working hard and we are doing all we can to practice what you teach us here, but I've been amazed at how fast he has healed, too. It's a miracle."

"Yes, I can see that," Lon said, nodding his head too.

"How are you feeling Jacob? Are you feeling any pain."

"I get tired after walking a long ways, but I can walk the length of our house and back without too much problem," Jacob explained.

"Let's see how things go, but I would say by next Monday, the 27th, you should be able to use your walker at school," Lon said, smiling at Jacob's expression. "I think with your mom being close, you could try it out and then ask her to bring your wheelchair if you need to rest."

"Yeah, we could try that," Amanda agreed. She was smiling about Jacob's excitement. She was pleased he was willing to go out in public with a walker, considering how much he disliked the idea at first.

They worked on core strengthening exercises and stretches for 30 minutes. Amanda joined in to help strengthen her core. Then they worked on Jacob's left arm. He was getting much stronger, and they did exercises that brought his arm above his head. These were different muscles than he used with his walker, but he was ready for the challenge.

Wednesday was their last visit to the Little Rock doctors. Amanda and Jacob got a small ice cream cone to celebrate the last nine-hour trip to Arkansas Children's Hospital. Amanda knew she wouldn't forget the team of people that saved Jacob's life. And she knew she wasn't going to be done paying for it for many years, but as she looked back at her 10-year-old son, it was worth it - every penny.

The rest of the week, Jacob got in a lot of practice with the walker. Jackson would walk with Jacob any time he practiced. Ally would race Jacob as he walked and excitedly shout she was faster. He just smiled at her as she boasted. He was glad he was even in the race. When he got in his electric wheelchair, he challenged her to another race and beat her by a scooter length. Everyone but Ally laughed about that one. Jacob let Ally sit in his lap and drive the electric wheelchair to make it up to her.

Monday morning came, and Jacob couldn't wait to go to school. Jackson carried Jacob's books to his first class, while he slowly shuffled along. Then Sabrina offered to help carry his books to his next class. After each class, friends were eager to help Jacob by carrying his stuff to the next class. By lunch time, however, he needed Amanda to bring up his wheelchair. He was getting too tired. Amanda had assumed that would be the case and encouraged him not to be discouraged. He had gone quite a while on the walker, and he was making a lot of progress. Jacob was pretty sore on Tuesday, so he used his wheelchair during the day before he went to physical therapy.

Lon congratulated Jacob on his progress and pushed Jacob with some new exercises.

"I know it's exciting to get stronger and start walking a lot," Lon said with a mock look of toughness. Jacob laughed. "But it's important not to forget about stretching and range of motion. Even bodybuilders like me, have to stretch so our bodies don't get sore and hurt again."

Jacob laughed louder at the idea of Lon being a body builder. Everyone laughed to see Jacob enjoying himself.

When they got home that night, Amanda spent some extra time helping Jacob stretch. He looked pretty worn out from all the exertion.

To Amanda's surprise, Jacob didn't wake up at all that night. She woke up twice to make sure Jacob was still breathing. She wished she could just sleep and trust she would wake up if he needed her. After more than two months of interrupted sleep, she was uncomfortable with more than three hours of sleep without checking on Jacob. She looked forward to getting used to it though.

Jacob used his walker again Thursday, though it was another short day of school due to physical therapy.

On Friday, Jacob used his walker the whole day. He walked slow and sat down as often as he could, but he was getting stronger too. Amanda still came up three times during the day to administer pain medicine, but Jacob had been able to take himself to the restrooms at school. He felt like he was almost back to normal. That made him beam with excitement.

By the time Jacob reached the end of school, he was exhausted. Amanda really had to help Jacob climb into the car. Jacob and Jackson talked about school around the dinner table and things they wanted to do on Saturday. They also talked about the upcoming deer hunting season. Jacob was sure he would be ready in time. He was still hoping to be ready to walk on his own by his birthday. It was only a week away.

Jacob went to bed a little early that night. Amanda saw how exhausted he was, and thought she might get a full night's sleep. She was worn out too, though she doubted her body would relax enough to go a whole night without waking up to check on Jacob.

Amanda went to bed at 11:00 pm and the next thing she knew the sun was rising in the east. She rushed to the boys room to check on Jacob. He was still asleep. Amanda felt like a new person. She had the first six hours of uninterrupted sleep since the incident. She was ready to go job hunting.

The boys played with Jacob's electric wheelchair for much of the morning. Amanda swept, mopped, and tidied up the house. When she called them in for lunch, Jacob rolled through the house and left a trail of muddy tire tracks in his wake. Jackson offered to help clean off Jacob's tires, then Amanda and Jackson cleaned up the floor. Jacob parked the electric wheelchair and used the walker the rest of the day.

On Sunday, Jacob decided to take his walker to church. When everyone saw Jacob walking in, they were filled with joy. Brother Ratley asked Amanda to tell everyone a little about their progress.

"As you can see, Jacob is walking with a walker, and before you know it, he will be walking on his own," Amanda said, tears coming to her eyes. "We have seen a miracle with his recovery, and we know that God has made it possible. Everyone has been so good to help us and very supportive. Thank you all. We flooded the gates of heaven with our prayers in July, and God has showered us with blessings ever since."

Everyone was touched, and there wasn't a dry eye in

the whole congregation. Everyone there had contributed something to help Amanda: meals, money, or service. Each had offered prayers on their behalf. It's not every day you see a miracle, and while it wasn't complete, they had tears of gratitude for what had already been done.

On Monday, Jacob was able to go to school and only called on Amanda twice. He just needed a little pain relief during the day. His friends continued to help carry his books. He hoped he would be able to carry his own books by Halloween.

Tuesday was shorter because of his physical therapy appointment. As they drove to the clinic, Amanda told Jacob this was the second to last appointment. Jacob didn't think they would stop going to therapy until he was walking on his own. He hoped today would be the day he got to walk without any support. He felt like he was so close.

Lon had Jacob walk on a treadmill, at the lowest setting so he could try lengthening his stride. Jacob still held onto the arm bars, and Lon stood behind Jacob to keep him steady. After only 10 or 15 seconds, Jacob started to lose his balance and Lon had to hold him up. Lon stopped the machine, and they went to different exercises. Lon didn't say anything about walking alone that day, and Jacob was upset that he didn't have better balance.

After they got home, Jacob walked with his walker - really trying to balance on his own without leaning on the walker. At school on Wednesday, he continued to focus on his balance and walking tall, even though it made him slower than before. He wanted to be ready to walk on his birthday.

Chapter 41
Cake Walk

Jacob had a big grin on his face as he left therapy the last day of September. It was the last session of physical therapy, but Amanda was pretty sure that wasn't why Jacob was so happy right now. It was also his 11th birthday, but Amanda knew it was more than that. She looked at Jacob in the rear view mirror and noticed the smile. She could almost guess why he was so happy.

"I'm very proud of you, Jacob," Amanda said, her smile almost as big as Jacob's. "You worked really hard at your physical therapy, and it shows in how far you have come. You've been blessed."

"Don't tell anyone though," Jacob said, making a semi-serious face at his mom. "I want to show brother before we tell him."

"I won't say anything," Amanda said, giggling with Jacob. She was anxious to see Jackson's face when he saw the good news.

They picked up Jackson and Ally at the babysitter's and drove to their house. Jacob couldn't talk or even look at his brother because he was worried he would give something away. When Amanda turned off the car, Jackson quickly went to the back of the Expedition and got Jacob's walker. Amanda helped Jacob ease down to the ground, and he grabbed the walker from Jackson like he usually did. Then Jacob looked at Jackson and said, "Look at this brother!" and he pushed the walker to the side and started walking towards the house.

Jackson stopped and stared. Each of Jacob's steps made Jackson smile a little more. After Jacob was halfway to the house, Jackson ran towards his brother, shouting for joy. Amanda grabbed the walker and put it back in front of Jacob after he had walked about 20 yards. After Jacob rested a minute, he hugged Jackson. Amanda wasn't sure which one was happier. But then again, maybe she was happiest of all. She had her kids together again at home, and it was almost normal. They had come so far.

"That was a pretty cool present Jacob gave you for his birthday," Amanda said to her kids. "Let's see if we can make his birthday a little more special. Don't tell anyone that comes tonight until we do the cake. Then when Jacob gets ready to blow out his candles, he can say, 'I wish I could walk without a walker.'"

"Then I'll stand up and start walking," Jacob said, finishing Amanda's thought. Everyone loved the idea and couldn't wait to have cake that evening.

It was a big group of family and friends that gathered for Jacob's birthday. Amanda kept Ally close by. She just knew that if someone started talking to Ally, the innocent four-year-old would tell the exciting news. Amanda didn't want Jacob's fun to be spoiled. As Amanda predicted, Ally almost told Granny and Eddy.

"We have some really good news," Ally began.

"We sure do," Amanda jumped in. "We have Jacob with us so we can celebrate another birthday. Isn't that wonderful?"

At the next available moment, Amanda reminded Ally it was their little secret that Jacob could walk without a walker. Ally remembered and put her hands over her mouth as she giggled.

Jacob seemed to walk a little slower than usual. Amanda briefly wondered if physical therapy had worn him out or maybe he was hurting, but Amanda saw that he was just trying to act like he needed the walker a little more than normal.

After the happy birthday song, Jacob said, "I wish I could walk again, without this dumb walker."

Then he blew out his candles. The applause was subdued, everyone not really sure what to do or say. They didn't have to wait long though. He pushed his walker to the side and walked ten paces over to his mother. This brought a wild applause and happy tears to many faces including Amanda's. Their struggles weren't over yet, but she was overjoyed that in just nine weeks, her son was walking again and well on his way to a normal life.

They enjoyed a lot of happy conversations with their family and friends for the next few hours. It was around 10:00 pm by the time Jacob got into bed. Amanda finished cleaning dishes and the kitchen before she went to sleep.

She hadn't been asleep for more than an hour when she heard Jacob cry out. She rushed to his bedside. Amanda knelt next to Jacob's bed and quickly tried to quiet him and see what was wrong so he wouldn't wake up his brother.

"I had a nightmare," Jacob said, fear marked every word. "No, it was real. It was a flood of bad memories."

"It's okay, Baby," Amanda said, wondering what this was about. "I'm here."

"I saw the day I got run over," Jacob said. Amanda's breath caught in her throat.

"I saw that I dropped the phone and when I reached over to pick it up, the wheels started to roll toward me and I fell," Jacob said, occasional sobs breaking in between his words. "I fell and said, 'Please God, don't let it hurt.' And then everything went black. I thought I was dead."

Amanda started to cry too, though she tried to keep it quiet. She just held her son, hoping she didn't need to say anything because she didn't know what to say.

"Then it got light again," Jacob said, the sobbing slowed and he started to relax a little. "I couldn't see anything, but it was pure white. I didn't hurt at all. I heard a voice say, 'Jacob, it isn't your time.' Then I said, 'But I want to stay here.'"

This was a new revelation to Amanda. She hadn't heard anything like this from Jacob before. She listened carefully and stopped crying.

"The voice said, 'You can't stay here. You have to go back,'" Jacob continued. "I asked, 'Why?' and he said, 'It isn't your time.' Then everything slowly turned back to black, and I never heard the voice again. The next thing I knew I woke up in dad's arms as he was putting me in the truck. I passed out again, and that's all I remember before waking up in the hospital."

"I'm sorry it scared you and woke you up," Amanda said with some difficulty. She wanted to be calm and reassuring for her son. "But I sure am glad it wasn't your time. I'm glad you got to stay with us."

Mother and son embraced in silence for a long time, until Jacob began to relax and fall asleep again. Amanda laid him down and then went back to her room. She knelt by her bed and thanked the Lord for saving her son and not taking him nine weeks ago. She hoped that tonight's dream was part of the healing process. It certainly was for her.

Chapter 42
Prolog

Amanda did get a job managing an office for a scrap yard that fall. It would be a couple years, but eventually, the farm insurance did what it was supposed to do and covered the doctor bills they incurred from the incident. Despite all the good care and miraculous healing Jacob received, he still deals with lingering pain and a few complications from the tractor incident.

Jacob got to go hunting and fishing and returned to many of the things he loved to do. In December, he and Amanda participated in a Christmas program for their church as a witness of the miracle in their lives and all those involved.

It took some time before Jacob could go into any kind of detail about the incident with anyone besides his mother. However, in May 2011, Amanda and Jacob participated in a Progressive Agriculture Safety Day. Safety Days are community events that teach school-age kids about safety on and around the farm. It often covers basic things like fire safety and first-aid, but it can also cover how to be safe around tractors and ATVs. This Safety Day focused on teaching fifth graders. Tammie Stutts coordinated the event and invited Jacob - with the help of Mom and Grandma - to share a simple account of his incident. He quickly shared what happened and encouraged kids not to play with cell phones around farm equipment and make sure the driver is paying attention when approaching a tractor vehicle. He was nervous about telling his story in front of his peers, but he saw that the kids were listening to him, which made it easier to drudge up the past.

Jacob returned to farming with his dad the following spring and continued to help out with some of the Safety Days over the next few years. At one of these Safety Days, he learned that a child colored a picture of his story, and how it made an impact in his life. Jacob was happy that he had helped some kids and families possibly avoid a similarly painful experience like his.

When asked how it impacted his relationship with God and his family, he said, "It's definitely made us closer. And now when we go through something difficult, we know we will get through it because we have been through worse before.

"I've always believed in God," Jacob continued. "I saw how He answered our prayers. I know I have to do my part, and He will do His."

For a long time, it bothered Jackson to talk about witnessing the incident with his brother. It's still difficult to relive the memories, but time has helped him cope with the experience.

"Every night I was praying and reading the Bible," Jackson said regarding how the incident impacted his relationship with God. "It got to the point where I wanted to go to church with whoever would go. I didn't know how God saved my brother, but I know He did it. Reading the Bible really helped me out. There were tons of things that happened in there that we can't explain, but it happened just the same."

Jacob and Jackson are still close in their teenage years. They enjoy different hobbies and run their own lives, but the bond that was strengthened in 2010 still binds them together today.

"Don't try to make me like my brother," Jacob said with a rye smile on his face. "I don't like it when people try to make us like each other."

"You say that, but you know you wouldn't let anything happen to your brother," Amanda said, softly chiding him.

"Oh, no one gets to mess with my brother but me," Jacob replied, the smile getting bigger. "That's my job."

The boys still call each other plain, old 'brother' most of the time. They are like many other brothers who don't really talk about feelings or sit around singing church songs together. But if ever there is trouble, they are side by side.

"I think knowing that we love each other made it easier to get through this experience," Jackson said. "I just wanted to help him get better and do anything I could for him.

Amanda has married again and has three stepchildren. They farm, run a construction company and do all the outdoor things they always enjoyed: hunting, camping, fishing, boating. The big thing is being together. Around mid-July, everyone is glad they have a miracle to celebrate, rather than a death to remember.

-- The End --

Thank you for reading Faith Through The Darkness! I hope you enjoyed it. If you did, please leave a review on Amazon, Goodreads or your favorite bookstore site.

You may also be interested in *Love Like Alzheimer's* - a novel about how a young couple faces the challenge of helping care for his grandma who has Alzheimer's disease. You will learn about the disease, how caregivers can cope and ways to take advantage of precious time with loved ones.

Go to Ryancurtisbooks.com to learn about more inspiring stories and books by Ryan Curtis.

Made in the USA
Middletown, DE
29 April 2020